how to have a
happy child

how to have a
happy child

Responding to your child's emotional needs from 4–12

Dr Richard C. Woolfson

hamlyn

An Hachette Livre UK Company

First published in Great Britain in 2007 by
Hamlyn, a division of Octopus Publishing Group Ltd
2–4 Heron Quays, London E14 4JP

Distributed in the United States and Canada by
Sterling Publishing Co., Inc.
387 Park Avenue South, New York, NY 10016-8810

ISBN-13: 978-0-60061-595-8
ISBN-10: 0-60061-595-2

Dr Richard C. Woolfson asserts his moral right to
identified as the author of this work.

A CIP catalogue record for this book is available from
the British Library

Contents

Introduction

Today's parents recognize the importance of happiness for their children. Doing well at school, having friends to play with, learning to play a musical instrument and owning lots of toys certainly help make life enjoyable for your child. But none of these means much unless he is happy.

Solid foundation

Happiness is the bedrock of your child's emotional development. A happy child looks forward to new experiences with enthusiasm, he enjoys each day as it unfolds and he thrives psychologically in each stage of his development. Naturally, there will be times when he is upset, for instance, when he is reprimanded by his teacher for talking instead of working, or when he loses his favourite toy or has a fight with his friend. These moments of distress are only temporary and will soon be submerged by his strong, underlying level of happiness.

In contrast, if he is miserable and discontented for much or all of the time, it won't matter how many toys he receives on his birthday or how many times he is taken to the cinema. The potential impact and pleasure to be gained from these activities is greatly reduced. Likewise, it doesn't matter how often he comes top of the class in school or how frequently he wins a sports trophy if his underlying mood is one of sadness. True, each of these experiences contributes in its own way to your child's happiness, yet they won't make him happy by themselves.

Sadly, evidence from research suggests that children are under more pressure than ever before these days, which means that a greater number of children are more stressed, unhappy and anxious than in previous generations – and that's another reason why you shouldn't take your child's happiness for granted any more.

Identifying happiness

Happiness is one of those psychological concepts that we recognize when we see it or experience it, but is hard to define. This book takes the view that your child's happiness constitutes his positive feelings of self-contentment, his positive feelings of emotional well-being and his positive feelings of satisfaction with himself, his attributes, his achievements and his relationships.

Sometimes his happiness is obvious, such as when his face breaks into a huge smile the moment he realizes you have come to pick him up from school, or when he laughs with excitement and delight while travelling on a plane to a holiday destination. His happiness is immediately evident on these occasions.

At other times, however, your child's happiness isn't so obvious. It could be expressed more subtly, for example, in his positive attitude to school. Although he might not tell you every single day that he is happy with his class work and school friends, and although he might not go to school each morning with a beaming grin across his face, his settled behaviour in class, his optimistic approach to homework, his excited chatter about his latest exploits in the school playground all tell you that he is happy with himself and with the world around him. As you get to know your child, you'll tune in to the very subtle signs that tell you whether or not he is happy or miserable.

How to have a happy child

There is no one 'right' way to raise a happy child. Much depends on your child's individual personality, temperament, skills and attitudes, your own approach to life and the relationship you and he have with each other. Even so, your child's happiness is not just a matter of chance and shouldn't be taken for granted. In most instances, it is achievable with your support and guidance.

This book considers many of the factors that can contribute positively to your child's general level of contentment. Beginning with a discussion about the development of happiness and the power of positive parenting, the book then examines the nature and

Satisfaction with himself, his achievements and relationships all contribute to a child's happiness.

importance of confidence. It follows with a detailed look at the ways in which your child can learn to manage his emotions more effectively, and goes on to explore those all-important social relationships. The final section focuses on the role of positive communication in developing happiness.

Covering the age range of 4 to 12 years, this is a comprehensive guide to help you steer your child towards a strong and sustainable level of happiness and self-contentment. As such, it is your essential parenting companion to raising happy children.

The happiness formula

Why happiness varies

You only need to look at a group of children to see that individuals experience different levels of happiness. One is bubbly and enthusiastic, while another is sad and glum-faced. Even within the same family, each sibling has her or his own level of contentment.

Taking control

On the opposite page is a list of the main factors that explain why some children are happier than others. Although these play a part and interact with each other to determine your child's happiness, the cause-and-effect relationship is not clear-cut. For example, a child who is very unpopular with her classmates and who therefore finds herself excluded from their games in the playground is likely to be unhappy. Yet a child who is dejected and down-hearted is unlikely to be invited by her peers to play with them. So it is hard at times to know whether it is the factor that influences the happiness or vice versa.

In any case, there is much that you can do to increase your child's contentment with herself and her life, irrespective of her temperament, bonding, relationships and experiences. Don't view happiness as a characteristic or emotional state that occurs passively – you can actively help your child develop happiness skills, that is, a variety of capacities that each have a positive impact on her emotional well-being. This book identifies these abilities, suggests ways in which you can teach them to your child and advises you on other strategies for boosting her happiness. There is no doubt that you can make a positive difference.

Happiness factors

Temperament Psychological research confirms that young babies have different personal traits, right from birth. For instance, some are easy to be with and are very settled – they feed, sleep and interact calmly and contentedly; others are difficult to manage, restless and generally ill at ease; and there are those who need plenty of time before reacting to stimulation from their carer. At the moment of arrival into this world, therefore, your baby's innate temperament affects her level of happiness.

Bonding The emotional connection that your baby forms with you – known as 'bonding' – has a huge impact on her happiness. A satisfactory emotional connection with at least one loving adult (such as her mother, father or carer) provides a bedrock for her

LEFT Children who play cooperatively find it easy to make friends and settle more quickly at school.

RIGHT A child who is excluded in the playground will be unhappy, making it less likely that she will be asked to join in.

future happiness to rest upon. It is the strength of that attachment that affects her later emotional and psychological development. Evidence suggests that a child who has not forged a positive bond by the age of three or four years will experience social difficulties throughout her life.

Relationships Your child's happiness is also influenced by her relationships with members of her family, with her peers and with other adults in her world. For example, a positive relationship with her siblings will increase her happiness, while jealousy and rivalry between them will reduce it. Likewise, a child who is popular is less likely to feel sad and miserable than a child who is socially isolated and rejected by her peers. By the age of five or six, the relationship she has with her teachers in school also determines her level of happiness.

Experiences Some life experiences are more damaging to a child's contentment than others. Losing a toy, for instance, will only have a temporary effect, whereas the death of a grandparent or parent will have a much more substantial impact. Your child's happiness is also influenced by her success in school, interactions with her peer group and moving home or school.

Happiness begins

Every child can be happy. However, the way in which happiness is achieved and expressed, tends to change as your child grows up. For example, what makes her happy at the age of four might have much less effect eight years later.

Ages and stages of happiness

The chart opposite explains how and why happiness develops through the years of childhood, but bear in mind that this is only an approximate guide, as individuals obviously vary from one to another.

In addition, your child's happiness is influenced by a variety of external factors that vary from individual to individual and from family to family. Therefore, not all children of the same age show their happiness in the same way, not is their happiness affected by the exact same influences. However, the chart will provide some guidance regarding what to expect of your child's happiness as she grows.

.

Each child expresses happiness in his or her own way – understandable given that events and personalities vary so widely.

What **makes** her happy

Aged 4   Your love and approval are important for your child's happiness at every age, but particularly so when she is younger, because relationships with peers have not fully formed. She is also delighted when she makes friends with other children, but friendships change frequently among four-year-olds.

Aged 6   Now that she is immersed in school life, her goals and aspirations have moved beyond family life. Happiness is connected more to peer-group relationships. Your approval of her achievements in school continue to matter to her, but your child also wants approval from her teacher. A reprimand in school may have more of an impact than a reprimand at home.

Aged 9   While your support and interest remain paramount to her well-being, friendships have become increasingly important as a potential source of happiness. Social experiences and popularity are valuable to her. With most children, achievement also assumes considerable significance, and her self-worth is highly influenced by the way she thinks others see her.

Aged 12   Peer acceptance and physical appearance become the biggest influences on her happiness. Your child wants to be one of the crowd, to wear the same clothes that her friends wear and to have the same material objects, but she also needs to know that you are there for her. Her self-confidence is easily shaken and you may find her happiness is quickly dented by a sarcastic remark.

How happiness **shows**

Aged 4   You know when she is happy, just from her body language. Her relaxed facial expression, her sparkling eyes, her laughter and her movement all tell you, 'I am absolutely delighted at the moment'. Verbal expressions of happiness are much less frequent at this tender age.

Aged 6   A vast increase in her language skills enables your six-year-old to express her happiness to you in words as well as in body language. She has the vocabulary and the language ability to tell you outright when she is happy or sad.

Aged 9   You can usually tell if she is happy by what she says or how she reacts to you. However, happiness derived from, say, attaining a good score in the latest class test may show in her calm sense of satisfaction rather than an overt display of emotion. Happiness has become a more complex issue.

Aged 12   Children aged 12 years or so can be very moody, apparently ready to lose their temper without any provocation. So what you think is a happy pre-teenager could turn out to be a volcano waiting to erupt!

POSITIVE PARENTING

Confident parenting

Confident parenting – believing in your own worth and ability – is good for you and for your child. He will be much happier when you feel good about yourself. Confident parenting also means having clear, fair and flexible discipline at home.

Self-doubt

The problem is that the responsibility of raising a child can be so overwhelming at times that you may start to have doubts about the way you manage your child, you might worry about your relationship with him and you may start to think that you are not as good a parent as you would like to be.

Remember, though, that confident parenting doesn't mean being right all the time. Listening to your child is important, too. You are not infallible. Sometimes children are able to offer their parents good suggestions about how disagreements can be resolved together – if you can agree fair rules with your child, it will be much easier for you both to follow through.

Boosting your confidence

Every parent has moments of self-doubt – that is perfectly normal. But when these moments become longer and longer periods of time, dominating your day from start to finish, then you need to take a more optimistic approach.

Remind yourself that every parent has times when they are uncertain about their skills. For example, there are plenty of very effective, loving parents who have difficulty settling their young child into school, perhaps because he is one of those who don't find it

A confident parent makes for a happier child – he knows where he stands and feels safe knowing you are in charge.

easy to make friends or maybe because the class teacher makes him anxious. Nobody progresses along the road of parenthood convinced that they are perfect parents.

Keeping an upbeat outlook

Here are some suggestions for ways to boost your confidence as a parent, so that both you and your child find life more enjoyable:

♡ **Don't feel guilty** There is nothing wrong in acknowledging that you are human, that you have weaknesses as well as strengths and that being a parent can be very hard work at times. Every parent experiences these feelings – you have nothing to feel guilty about. True, there will be some aspect of caring for your child that you could have carried out more effectively, but he won't even have noticed.

Listen to your child when you have disagreements – you may be surprised at the solutions for resolving differences.

♡ **Maintain perspective** Don't get things out of proportion. As a parent, every single day is full of decisions that have to be made, packed with judgements about what to do best for your child. Sometimes you will make a good decision and at other times you will wish you had taken a different approach. But in most instances these are minor matters that have no long-term negative impact on your child's development.

♡ **Talk to your partner, family member or friend** Discuss your self-doubts with the person closest to you. You will feel much more positively once you have voiced your concerns. A word of reassurance from them may be just what you need to feel more confident about yourself. And be prepared to listen to any praise offered to you – you may be surprised to discover that other people think that you are coping admirably. It's amazing how a positive comment from someone can significantly boost your self-esteem as a parent.

♡ **Focus on your strengths** One of the effects of low self-confidence is that you start to interpret all your behaviour negatively. You can break this cycle, however, by forcing yourself to identify your strengths, such as the way you comforted him the last time he was upset. Try to spend more time thinking about your strengths and achievements as a parent rather than on your perceived weaknesses.

♡ **Accept help** Parenting should be shared with your partner, close family member or friend whenever possible. Aside from close family and friends, there may be other friends and relatives able to give you a helping hand every now and again. Accept such offers of support with open arms when they are given to you. You will feel refreshed and stronger, even after a break that lasts only half an hour, and you will find that your self-confidence has improved too. Learning to accept help from others also helps you recognize that you don't need to do everything on your own, that you can benefit from others.

The right balance

Raising a happy child is a balancing act. You constantly have to weigh up choices in order to decide what's best for your child. Some of these choices are relatively minor, while others are more significant.

Making choices

Sometimes you find yourself having to make choices that are in the best interests of your child, even though such choices seem to go against your own interests – like when your child asks permission to stay at her friend's house. If you are only thinking of yourself, you would probably refuse her request because you will have to go and collect her when you would rather be at home relaxing. If you are only thinking of her, you will probably agree to her request because she will have fun and will strengthen the relationship with her friend.

Sensible parenting may involve making some choices that cause unhappiness – balancing everyone's needs can be hard.

Everybody counts

Striking a balance as a parent requires you to take account of everybody's interests, which may occasionally conflict. Be honest with yourself. When weighing up the pros and cons of a parenting choice, try to clarify whose interest you are considering. If you realize that you always put your needs before those of your child, you could start to make different choices.

Avoid extremes

Children often seek extremes, especially as they move into the double-digit years. For instance, many 12-year-olds will rush to the most thrill-generating activity at the theme park, and many ten-year-olds will

Ask your child what she thinks about the decisions you have made and be prepared to listen.

try to ride their bicycle as fast as they can. Extremes are exciting for most children, but that doesn't mean living on the edge is good for them. In fact, as a general parenting principle, you should assume that your child thrives best in the middle ground.

When thinking about strategies for use with your child aim for a balance between extremes, no matter how much you may be tempted to go right up to the limits. It comes down to knowing your child's individual strengths and weaknesses, learning from past experience what she reacts most positively to and then striking a balanced parenting approach. That is the best way to promote your child's happiness.

The middle way Research shows that child development is most satisfactory when discipline at home is neither too punitive nor too lax. In other words, a fair system of rules that involves a combination of appropriate rewards and punishments is better than either no rules at all or an excessive amount of punishment and rewards. The same theory also applies to studying for school tests.

Key questions

When trying to achieve a balance in the way you manage your child, ask yourself the following questions:

• Does my parenting seem extreme compared to other parents?

• How does my child react when I push her to the limits?

• Do my own interests often conflict with my child's interests?

• How willing am I to allow her something she wants, even though I disagree?

• What impact do my parenting strategies have on my child's development?

• Am I prepared to modify the way I raise my child in the light of experience?

• Are my ideas about how to parent fixed and unchanging?

• How often do I ask my child for her views on decisions that I have to make?

A harsh study schedule that involves too many hours pouring over books at home will make your child sad and this will interfere with her learning, while no study at all will create anxiety because she eventually realizes that the exam will be too challenging for her. A balanced study schedule that combines work and play will generally produce an optimal outcome.

Emotional intelligence

Your child's emotional intelligence – that is, his awareness of his own feelings and the feelings of other people, and the competent way in which he controls and manages these emotions – makes a significant contribution to his happiness.

Inborn and acquired

An emotionally intelligent child has an honest awareness of his moods and is reasonably capable of controlling them; at the same time, he is sensitive to the varying feelings of those around him, whether children or adults. This emotional harmony and understanding raises your child's sense of well-being and contentment. As with virtually all psychological traits, your child's level of emotional intelligence is almost certainly a combination of the sensitivity he was born with, the emotional skills that he learns while growing up and the interaction between these innate and acquired abilities. Therefore, the fact that

some children seem to be born with more potential for emotional intelligence than others does not mean that this potential is fixed. Parenting, family life, experiences at home and in school and relationships with friends and siblings all play a part in nurturing emotion intelligence.

Verbalizing feelings

There are many dimensions of emotional intelligence that you can encourage in your child, and these will be specifically discussed later in this book, for instance, self-control, a positive attitude, self-confidence, motivation and empathy. But as well as targeting these individual characteristics in particular, there are general strategies you can implement at home, such as encouraging him to express his feelings through words rather than through behaviour.

A younger child often has more difficulties verbalizing his feelings than an older child, largely because, say, a four-year-old's language skills are less advanced than those of a 12-year-old. That is why you may need to give him lots of time and support when encouraging him to talk to you about emotional topics. Let your child know that you want to understand what he feels inside, explain that you will

Foster emotional intelligence at home by listening and by helping him to find the words that express his emotions.

Girls tend to be more empathetic in relationships and may comfort a tearful friend from quite an early age.

help him put his emotions into words and be patient as he slowly learns to express himself through spoken language instead of body language.

Bear in mind that you can't force your child to have a more mature level of emotional intelligence. However, there is evidence from research that emotional intelligence can be enhanced by creating a home framework around the child that recognizes the importance of understanding each other's feelings. Your child's emotional development continues through the early years and into adolescence, and this means that your input during these formative years counts. If he becomes sensitive, caring and thoughtful towards others during childhood, he is likely to continue to be like that as an adult.

QUESTIONS & ANSWERS

Q Are there differences between boys and girls when it comes to emotional intelligence?

A Yes, there are some differences between the sexes. For instance, girls (compared to boys) tend to have more empathy and understanding, and also tend to be more aware of the emotional dimensions of friendships. Yet boys (compared to girls) are generally more effective when it comes to coping with stress; also, they typically have higher levels of self-confidence. Psychologists claim that girls and boys have the same potential for emotional intelligence – it's just that their specific strengths lie in different areas of this characteristic.

Q What can I do to nurture my child's emotional intelligence?

A Aside from working on specific dimensions, aim to generate a 'listening' environment at home, one in which your child is able to express his feelings in the full knowledge that he will be listened to, and have discussions about emotions. Encourage him to consider the feelings of his friends and his siblings when he plays with them. You will go a long way to nurturing emotional intelligence by creating an atmosphere at home in which awareness of feelings is high on the agenda. And of course, set a good example yourself.

Juggling different needs

Every child is different in terms of their personality, characteristics, interests and abilities. However, each child has the same basic emotional needs, including the need to be loved and feel valued, safe and secure, as well as the need to be stimulated within a caring environment.

Prioritizing needs

Your child's development depends on these psychological needs being satisfied, yet it is hard to say which emotional need has greater priority over others. Certainly the need to have a close emotional attachment is fundamental to your child's ability to form social relationships with children and adults; and she also needs to be loved and to feel secure. Yet her other emotional needs are important too. For instance, if her need for stimulation isn't met, she will fail to achieve her maximum potential. And if she doesn't feel valued by those around her, her self-confidence will drop. Her sense of safety and security is also important for her development. All her emotional needs matter in their own way.

Emotional needs and happiness

There is a direct link between emotional needs and happiness. A child whose emotional needs are not met will be miserable and unhappy because she won't feel good about herself, she won't feel cared for and she won't feel safe. Happiness is built upon a general feeling of psychological well-being, which won't be present if she is emotionally dissatisfied. In contrast, happiness is much more likely to prevail when your child is raised in a loving, caring home life that is sensitive to her changing emotional needs.

Meeting your child's emotional needs – to feel loved, valued and secure – happens naturally in a loving family environment.

Identifying emotional needs

In most cases, parents instinctively know to meet their child's emotional needs. For instance, you know to cuddle your four-year-old when she cries, you know to help your ten-year-old with her homework when she struggles with it and you know to tell your 12-year-old how proud you are when she is kind towards her little brother. These are all spontaneous ways in which you attend to her psychological requirements without even thinking about it.

Getting it right

You will recognize when her emotional needs are not being met – you will be able to tell by her behaviour, manner and language. An insecure child will be nervous, anxious and afraid of new challenges; an under-stimulated child will eventually become passive, bored and lethargic; and a child who feels unloved may express her resentment about this by fighting with her peers, either verbally or physically. Although not every psychological problem can be attributed to unmet emotional needs, this can be a significant factor.

Juggling all these different needs is not as a difficult as it sounds. For most of the time, you won't have to think about it – you will find that just by creating a loving family environment, your child's emotional development progresses satisfactorily. However, there may be instances when there is an indication that one of her emotional needs isn't being met, for example, when your nine-year-old reveals to you that she thinks you don't appreciate how hard she tries in school. When that happens, look at the situation candidly and address her needs directly.

Try to take a long-term view. For example, don't panic when you see a single episode of her unhappiness – that's probably an immediate reaction to a temporary problem. However, you would be justifiably concerned about her emotional needs if she appears miserable over a longer period.

As parents, our emotional impulses towards our children are often right – instinctively we cuddle a tearful toddler.

Excessive emotional needs

There are some children who appear to have demanding emotional needs that are disproportionate to normal expectations. If your child falls into this category, rather than simply responding each time she demands attention, ask yourself why she might feel this way. Perhaps she feels threatened by your new baby, or maybe she feels insecure because she has few friends. Try to identify the underlying pressure that could cause this excessive need for attention.

Confidence

The 'can-do' child

A 'can-do' child has so much self-belief that he launches himself into new challenges with the total conviction that he is going to succeed. He is not arrogant — he simply has a positive, optimistic attitude.

Maximizing achievement

The 'can-do' child sees opportunities, not obstacles; experiences challenges, not hurdles; visualizes achievement, not failure; and loves the thrill of new learning. The 'can-do' 11-year-old looks forward to the new maths lesson because he is confident that he can cope, and the 'can-do' five-year-old relishes the prospect of his friend's birthday party because he loves the excitement of mixing with others. It is not just that all 'can-do' children are extremely talented, capable and high-achievers; some are, but many are just average children who are able to maximize their potential as a result of their positive attitude.

When he 'can't do'

In contrast, the 'can't-do' child expects to fail, makes excuses, doesn't get on well with his friends, dreads new experiences and typically makes very disparaging remarks about himself — he willingly tells everyone how hopeless he is and how worthless his attainments are (even if they are good). Consequently, the 'can't-do' child has an uphill struggle with all aspects of his everyday life, he has less pleasure, is more tense and has fewer friends.

A confident child is equipped to deal with the challenges and adventures of life, and actively loves to learn.

What to **do**

Make your child feel special. You can boost his self-belief by taking an interest in everything he does, by letting him know how pleased you are with his progress and achievements by spending time with him whenever you can.

Give encouragement. It is not easy for your child to persist at an activity that he finds too difficult, so be prepared to spur him on. Your words of encouragement might be just what he needs to boost his confidence.

Break challenges into small stages. He is much more likely to develop a 'can-do' belief in himself when he is able to break one large task into several smaller steps – for example, tidying his room is easier if he sorts it out one section at a time.

Maintain consistent discipline at home. There is evidence from psychological research to suggest that a child has higher self-belief when his parents use structured discipline, with a balance of rewards and punishments.

Be a 'can-do' parent. Your attitude rubs off on your child, so if he sees you, for instance, approach work-based problems with confidence, he will try to do the same. He also learns coping strategies from watching you tackle problems positively.

What **not** to do

Don't focus on his weaknesses. Whenever his confidence sags because he thinks he is not as capable as he would like to be, encourage him to think of all his positive characteristics, such as his pleasant personality or his good sense of humour.

Don't make fun of him. The challenge facing him may seem easy to you because you are an adult with lots of experience, but it doesn't look that way to your child. Listen to his self-doubts, take them seriously and provide him with reassurance, then discuss ways in which he can overcome any difficulties.

Don't allow negative self-talk. When he has self-doubts, he may start to describe himself in negative terms. And if he expects to fail, very soon he will fail. Discourage him from making pessimistic remarks about his abilities.

Don't solve everything for him. By all means talk through possible ways forward with your child when he is unsure what to do. However, don't always find the solution for him; instead, lead him to a successful strategy that he hadn't thought of before.

Don't skimp on praise. Your approval and affirmation of his self-worth encourage him to persist and boost his 'can-do' attitude. Your praise may also help him recognize his own achievements, which he might otherwise just take for granted.

Expectations

Your child wants to live up to your expectations – that is only natural. She needs your approval and she also needs to know that you believe in her. But make sure that your expectations are not set too high, otherwise she is doomed to fail.

Keeping it real

Setting clearly defined goals may have many potential advantages, but they will be lost if they are unrealistic, in other words, if they demand far too much of your child. Even if she starts out with the intention to achieve them, she will soon realize that they are beyond her abilities. The net effect will be lack of enthusiasm, lack of motivation, apathy, passivity and a sense of failure. The challenge for you is to set a target for your child that is ahead of the present stage in her development, yet not so advanced that it is totally beyond her reach.

For instance, there is no point in setting a target for your four-year-old to tie her shoelaces in a tight, well-balanced bow. No matter how hard she tries, the task is almost certainly beyond her at this age because she doesn't have the muscle power, the finger control or the hand-eye coordination to tie her shoelaces properly. Any attempt to do so will result in frustration, tears and a drop in happiness. Match the goal to your child's development, not to the development you would like her to have.

How to set a realistic goal

To achieve their maximum effect, goals for your child should be:

Small Aim for little steps in progress rather than huge jumps; a good strategy is to divide a large target or task into several small steps, leading on from one another.

Understandable She should know exactly what it is she is aiming for; that way, her mind will be focused and her efforts will be purposeful.

Set realistic goals for your child and before long the training wheels will be off and she'll be flying along.

Agreed Goals should be decided jointly between you and your child; she is more likely to show commitment when she is involved in setting them.

Realistic There is no point in asking her to achieve the impossible; an attainable goal harnesses her intrinsic desire to improve.

Measurable Your child should know when she has reached her target; it should be expressed in precise terms so that she knows when it is achieved.

Goal management

When setting purposeful goals for your child, think about whether they are in your child's interests, the family's interests or both – obviously avoiding any conflict of interest is important for family harmony. Make sure that these goals make sense in the light of her current level of psychological development and assess to what extent achieving them will improve your child's life in some way. Also, see if you can build in a way for you to work with your child to reach the target. You then need to plan ahead to consider how you might support your child if she does not achieve her target. And if she does reach her aim, what will the follow-on goal be, or do you see this goal as one part of a larger goal?

Supporting achievement

It helps to use lots of praise and encouragement to ease her towards the agreed goal. However, be careful of overdoing it. Push the right amount and your child will feel that you support her; push her too hard and she will feel resentment towards you. The best way to avoid asking too much of your child is to monitor her progress towards the goal very carefully. Talk to her regularly about this. As she progresses towards her target, you will see her confidence levels rise and her happiness increase. Celebrate her successes with her.

Targets that can be broken down into achievable stages will make goals more attainable – give lots of encouragement.

Setting targets

Having clear targets or goals for your child is extremely helpful, whether the target for your eight-year-old is to go to bed by a certain time each night, or for your 12-year-old to be polite to her younger brother during mealtimes. Goals can give a huge lift to your child's confidence because they:

- Present a clear target for her to aim at.

- Ensure that you and your child know what she is trying to achieve.

- Typically have a motivating effect on her.

- Enable her to know exactly when she has succeeded.

- Facilitate better concentration on the main task.

Recognizing individuality

There are lots of children the same age as your child, but no matter how many others match her in some ways, she remains unique. It is her particular mixture of personal traits that differentiates her from everyone else; that is what makes her so special.

Individual interests

Developing and enhancing your child's individuality is easier said than done because there are a number of practical constraints that work against this approach. For example, if you buy a piano for your eldest child, you will find it more convenient for your next child to learn to play the piano rather than having to buy another expensive musical instrument. Consequently, she ends up learning to play the piano even if that doesn't match her individual interests. Then there are your own aspirations for your child about the sort of education you want her to have, and the type of career you would like her to follow, but these may clash with her individual skills and interests. This can result in your child's individuality being undermined.

Resisting peer pressure

One of the biggest external challenges to your child's individuality, from the age of seven or eight onwards, is peer pressure; that is the psychological pressure for her to be like her friends. At times her need to be part of the group can be so strong that she is willing to put her own tastes and preferences aside, just so that she conforms to others' expectations. Encourage your child to defend her personal beliefs, even when that runs the risk of causing unpopularity. She mustn't be afraid to be an individual.

Every child has their own interests, talents and aptitudes. The challenge is to match this uniqueness with suitable activities.

Nuturing her individuality

Take the following steps to identify the various elements of your child's individuality, and nurture and support those unique, positive qualities day to day:

♡ **Take stock of her individuality** Make a point of standing back from the pressures of everyday life in order to see who your child really is. What is it about her that makes her so different from everyone else? Blot out other distractions and concentrate only on your child and her particular qualities. This will help you build a clearer picture.

♡ **Appreciate her strengths** Perhaps you could describe your child's strengths at a moment's notice, but it won't do you any harm to sit down and spend a couple of minutes making a written list of her desirable traits and abilities.

♡ **Encourage her interests** Supporting your child's individuality also involves providing stimulation and activities that allow her to express and develop her personal interests. Without such opportunities, her uniqueness cannot flourish. So think about what your child is most interested in and what you can do to nurture those interests.

♡ **Praise her achievements** Consider the extent to which you acknowledge your child's individual progress. Your approval of her attainments in all her endeavours, whether academic, sporting or creative, matters a lot to her. She needs to know that you are proud of what she has managed to attain in all areas of her life.

♡ **Resist comparing her to others** Maybe it would be better in some respects if your child was more like her older brother, for instance, but comparing her to him will only make her feel that her individuality is a problem, not an asset, and her

Learning to play the piano may be fine for one of your children, but another might prefer the trombone or drums.

happiness will fall. Avoid measuring your child against other children in any circumstances.

♡ **Encourage her talents** Do your best to maximize your child's potential, no matter what area that might involve – even if it is something outside your own interests. Perhaps, for example, you would prefer her to aspire to be a doctor rather than an actor, but her talent could lie in theatre and drama.

Feelings of self-worth

Your child's self-confidence is so important to his happiness. If he feels good about himself, then life seems so much better. And this applies as much to when he is four years old as it does to when he is 12 years old – confidence adds to his enjoyment of his everyday experiences.

Sympathetic support

Even children who are normally brimming with self-confidence can have days when a challenge seems insurmountable or they are afraid of reprimand, ridicule and humiliation. Always listen to your child's fears. Even though you may not agree with him when he tells you that he is afraid to try because every other pupil in his class is brighter than him, let him tell you this anyway and provide a sympathetic ear. Once you have listened, encourage him to at least try. The chances are that his performance will turn out to be better than he anticipated.

A sympathetic ear and kind words are as welcome to a sad four-year-old as they are to any adult. Listen and encourage.

Measured and positive approach

You can increase your child's confidence when he has to learn a new skill by breaking it down into small steps, each one progressing slightly from the previous one. For instance, the first stage in learning to ride a bicycle could be for him to sit on the bike, hands on the handlebars, while you hold it steady for him. The next step could be for him to sit on the bike while you push it along the road; and so on until he can turn the pedals without any support.

Always take a positive line. You may feel annoyed with his reluctance to try something new, but don't let your irritation show. Far better to coax him gently, all the time reassuring him that he will eventually succeed. This is the way to ensure that he tries everything at least once.

What you can **do**

Emphasize his strengths. Whenever he explains that he won't try something new because he lacks the necessary skills to achieve it, encourage him to think about all his strong characteristics. Point out the previous times he eventually succeeded.

Avoid comparisons. You may be tempted to encourage him to try something new by comparing him to his sisters and brothers, but this strategy will probably only make matters worse. It is best to treat him as an individual.

Involve him in decisions. Your child feels more confident about himself and his skills when he is allowed to make decisions for himself. Decision-making empowers him, lifting his self-confidence and increasing his happiness level.

Praise him and his achievements in front of other people. Affirmation from others boosts his confidence too. He likes to receive positive feedback from anyone whom he values, whose opinion he relies upon.

Point out to him how far he has advanced since the last time. He needs you to highlight how much further on he is this week than last week, as he may not notice such small changes himself.

What you can **say**

'I know you can do it. Do you remember when you had to learn something like this the last time, but you managed to do it anyway? You have the ability and I'm sure that when you try, you'll find that it isn't a problem.'

'Just do the best you can. Don't worry about what the others are doing – that doesn't matter. What matters is how hard you try, not how you compare with anyone else. I'll be proud of you because you're so special.'

'I'm not sure what to do about this. What would you like to happen? I'll explain the choices you can make and then you and I can talk about it until we reach a decision that we both agree on. You'll enjoy that.'

'I can't wait to tell your grandmother about how well you did in your class test. She'll be so proud of you. She thinks you are terrific and she will be delighted to hear how well you have done. You should be proud of yourself.'

You've made so much progress since the last time. Do you remember when you first tried to do this a couple of weeks ago that it was so difficult? Now see how much you can do. You'll make even more progress in the next couple of weeks.

Using play positively

Play remains a serious business as far as your child is concerned. Not serious in the sense that he has a frown on his face (although play can be dogged with frustration, embarrassment and irritation), but serious in the sense that play makes a significant contribution to the development of his happiness and self-confidence.

Why play is special

Aside from the sheer pleasure he derives from playing with his latest computer game or the new toy he received for his birthday, he also enjoys mixing with his friends, overcoming challenges and learning new skills. Then there is the thrill of adventure when he builds a den in the garden, for example. All of these experiences add to your child's happiness. You can't put a price on the smile of self-confidence that radiates from his face the first time he rides his bicycle without any additional supports.

Changing interests

His interests in play change as he grows older. What matters is that your child is able to play with the toys and games that fire his enthusiasm. This might be the latest electronic game, or it could the construction set that he has played with for years. Bear in mind that he may experience pressure from his friends to drop pretend-play because they regard it as 'babyish', even though he secretly loves using his imagination in that way. Help him to have the confidence to follow his play interests. Children who are 12 years old play different games from four-year-olds, but they still play!

Playing with your child

It is easy to fall out of the habit of playing with your children as they grow older, but getting the whole family involved can be a great boost to your child's happiness. Whether it is a ball game in the park or a board game at home on a rainy day, spending quality time with your children is important. Of course, arguments may break out between siblings, but the risk is worth taking for the opportunity to have everyone interacting together and enjoying each other's company. Your child's enthusiasm will lift when he sees that you also have fun playing with him.

LEFT AND BELOW Continue to play with your children as they grow; whether board game or ball game, they will revel in the attention and the fun.

Q When my child tries to assemble one of his large jigsaws, he often ends up in tears of frustration and anger at the challenge. How can that possibly make him happy?

A At his age, play involves a range of emotions because it is often very demanding. That is why he has those moments of anguish. But these pale into insignificance compared to the happiness he achieves from slipping the last piece of the jigsaw into place. You know exactly what he feels when he calls out proudly, 'Come and see this, I've finished it!'

Q My six-year-old son has asked for a doll for his birthday. I'm afraid he will be teased for being effeminate. Should I try to discourage him?

A If you make an issue of gender differences in play, you risk denting your child's self-confidence. No child ever suffered psychological harm simply from playing with a toy designed for the opposite sex. If you refuse to let your child play with a game or toy simply on the grounds of sex, you can create self-doubts and make him feel anxious. Take an even-handed approach wherever possible. Bear in mind that your child should have a wide range of play activities to help him develop his happiness and self-confidence to the maximum. Children can be highly critical on any number of counts, so if your child is teased, you need to help him deal with it in the same way that you would in any other situation.

Creative thinking

Children think in different ways. Some are analytical, while others are creative. Both styles can be effective, but creative thinking involves more risk-taking and is often more exciting. Your child will feel happy with the results when she engages in creative thinking.

Removing barriers

In your child's natural desire to find the right answer as quickly as possible, she instinctively puts up a number of psychological barriers to creative thinking, such as:

'I know how it's used.' She looks at an object, such as a chair, and immediately assumes that it is to be used for sitting on. This assumption closes her mind to other possibilities, for example, using it for shelter or standing on it.

'It's not going to work.' Your child's growing understanding of the world around her instinctively encourages her to root her ideas in reality, which means that she isn't always able to think flexibly. She pre-judges her ideas in terms of the practicality she knows.

'It's a silly idea.' Peer acceptance is very important, especially once she has started school. She wants to be popular with her classmates and the desire for social approval inhibits her ability to think independently and freely.

'It's good already.' True, the world is full of useful objects that have been developed by brains sharper than that of your child. Yet such a belief can exclude her from perceiving the potential for improvement on what already exists.

Encourage your child to use creative thinking – it's more risky than analytical thought, but it can be more fun.

The more she thinks creatively, the more confidence she will have to try the next time. Therefore, talk to her about these psychological barriers to creative thinking – making her aware of them will have a positive effect because she was probably not conscious of them before. Encourage her to make a deliberate effort to overcome those self-imposed hurdles to creative thinking.

Games you can **play**

How can that be used? A good mind-stretching activity to play with your child, just to broaden her perspective on thinking, is to ask her to think of uses for certain objects. It doesn't matter if they are silly uses, practical uses or helpful uses.

How can that be improved? This mind game requires your child to devise ways in which everyday objects could be improved in some way. Besides expanding her thinking, both of you are sure to have lots of fun playing this game together.

How does it look upside down? This strategy is designed to encourage your child to think creatively about the world around her by asking her to look at ordinary situations in her life from the opposite way round.

What crazy ideas have you got? In this group activity, participants are asked to contribute any ideas they want to, while suspending judgement (they can't criticize anybody's idea) and accepting without question what anyone else says (they can't reject concepts on the grounds of impracticality).

How the game **works**

Pick an everyday object of your choice and ask her to think of, say, 50 different uses for it. Set a time limit of around five minutes for her to complete the list. What matters is that she begins to think beyond the usual boundaries that she sets herself.

Draw up a list of ordinary household objects and ask your child to think of ways in which they could be improved. For instance, a book could be given a rubber cover so that it doesn't make a noise when it is dropped on the floor, or a table could have hydraulic legs so that it can be instantly adjusted to match the height of those using it. It doesn't matter how ambitious or bizarre the ideas are – it is her chance to think inventively.

Ask your child to imagine that, instead of going to school each morning, she could stay at home and the school could come to her, for example. The teacher could bring the books, lessons and other pupils to her bedroom, while she lies in bed! Don't worry if the opposite approach seems impractical or stupid – let her imagination run free.

Encourage the participants to come up with unusual suggestions and try to link different ideas together, even where there is no obvious connection between them. Your child could sit with three or four of her friends and spend ten minutes creating ideas for, say, a new way of travel that is totally eco-friendly.

Coping with failure

Children are so fragile when it comes to failure. Maybe your ten-year-old was buoyant when he left home this morning, but was totally dejected when he returned, after hearing that he had failed to be picked for the school running team. In most instances, failure hurts.

Reluctance to try

You need to help him bounce back from failure – if you don't, he may grow afraid to tackle anything new. The danger is that the prospect of failure starts to loom large in his mind. Soon he doesn't have any belief in his own abilities, and as a result he becomes reluctant to try an activity unless he knows for certain that he will succeed. And he may make highly critical observations of himself; for instance, he may ridicule his own art work, even though in reality his paintings are good. Repeated failure can reduce his motivation completely, which in turn increases the likelihood of even more failure.

Positive approach

It is true that some children are remarkably sure of themselves, even though they have no reason to be, for example, the child who is poorly coordinated and yet always wants to play a forward position in a soccer game. Such cases are marvellous to witness, but there are common-sense limits, and such a child could find himself at the wrong end of the popularity scale. Step in with clear advice to your child if you think this is about to happen to him.

Your child bounces back from failure only when he believes in himself and in his talents. He also has to like himself. Part of this self-confidence stems from

LEFT AND ABOVE Not eveyone can win all the time and helping your child to cope with failure, and take it in his stride, is as important as winning.

your relationship with him. If he feels that you care for him, that you are interested in him, that you love him and value him, then he will feel more able to meet failure head on.

Self-comparison

Your child's own perception of himself in relation to other children his own age also matters. Just as you compare yourself to your friends, so too does your child. He wants to be at least as effective as everyone else his age, and at least as popular. Through this process of self-comparison he learns about his strengths and weaknesses, his talents and his limitations. And if the result of this process of comparison disappoints him, then his happiness starts to ebb away. All it takes to dent his confidence is for him to realize, for example, that he can't climb as high on the climbing frame as his friend, or that he can't ride a bicycle as well as the others

? QUESTIONS & ANSWERS

Q My child sings at the top of his voice, but he's totally out of tune. Should I tell him to sing more quietly?

A While you should not suggest that he hides his tuneless singing voice – after all, he thinks that singing is good fun – there's no harm in gently pointing out that, although you might enjoy listening to his musical voice, others may not be so enthusiastic about it. You have to strike a balance between a realistic appraisal of his singing skills and making him want to give up singing altogether. Handled sensitively, however, this can be achieved.

Q My child never gets chosen for a part in the school play and his self-confidence is plummeting. What can I do to help?

A For a start, help him practise and rehearse in preparation for an audition. Work with your child to improve his acting skills, as best as you can. You may even decide to enrol him in drama lessons so that he has some more training before it's time for the next school play. Encourage him to try again despite previous failures. The fact that he has failed on previous occasions doesn't mean that he should give up. Persuade him to have another go, and keep supporting him until he succeeds or finds a different challenge.

Decision-making

You spend your life protecting your child, keeping him safe and making decisions that will ensure his best interests. Yet you can't make all his decisions for him forever – there comes a point when you have to start sharing that responsibility with your growing child.

Let her choose which pair of shoes to wear; it's a small thing but allows her to learn the skill of decision-making.

Time to start

You need to involve your child in decisions at some point to enable him to cope when you are not with him. It is not easy letting your child go solo, but you have to trust and encourage your child to make simple, safe and independent decisions. Begin this process when he is only four or five years old. Start off small. Build up your child's confidence and decision-making skills by allowing him to make minor choices in his life. For example, if he is young, let him choose between two breakfast cereals each morning or to select which shoes to wear at the weekend. These are relatively unimportant judgements, but they give your growing child early experience of making decisions. The more he does this, the better his self-confidence when it comes to thinking independently.

Teaching decision-making skills

When you make a choice in your life, you look at all the alternatives and weigh up the pros and cons of each possibility very carefully. There is no reason why you can't encourage your child to do the same, to think carefully about the impact of his decisions. Discuss with him why he chose this one instead of that one. Do this in a friendly, open way, otherwise your child will assume that you are critical of his decisions. Let him explain the rationale behind his selection, even though you might not agree with his final choice. Conversations of this kind encourage your child to evaluate the options very carefully – a process that should underpin all his decision-making.

Decisions in context

Help your child to develop the ability to make appropriate decisions within the situations in which he finds himself in the following ways:

♡ **Encourage him to consider the implications** Every choice your child makes affects others in the family, so suggest that he considers the impact of his choices on his siblings and on you. That is part of family life.

♡ **Set limits on his choices** Obviously you need to set limits on the range of choices available to your child so that there is no misunderstanding. There is no point in letting him consider an option that isn't possible or practical.

♡ **Be prepared for differences of opinion** If you do allow him to choose, remember that he might make an independent decision that is different from the choice you would really like him to make. Be ready for him to differ from you.

♡ **Follow the decision through** It is pointless telling your 12-year-old that he has a free choice when you don't actually mean it. Only tell him that he has a choice when you are genuinely willing to let him make the decision.

♡ **Steer him away from self-doubt** Human nature makes us automatically have doubts about the choice we have made, and your child will probably have the same post-decision anxieties too. But encourage him to take a positive outlook.

Making small decisions from an early age helps your child analyse the pros and cons of the alternatives on offer.

Decision-making example

The decision Suppose, for instance, that your nine year-old can't decide whether to wear his new trainers for playing in the muddy park.

Making it Ask him to think what it would mean to put on his new footwear (for instance, he would be delighted to wear them, but would be sad if they got dirty quickly) and to put on his old trainers (for example, he would be disappointed not wearing them to the park, but would be pleased because they would still be in pristine condition when going out with his friends at the weekend). Weighing up the facts like this – even when the decision is trivial – helps your child reach an informed choice.

Spotting possibilities

Your child's satisfaction with herself is closely linked to the amount of control she thinks she exerts. She is pleased when she knows that she can do something to make a situation better. In contrast, if she feels helpless to improve the situation, she is downcast and frustrated.

Seeing the openings

Recognizing possibilities for change gives her that essential sense of mastery and control in her life. Suppose, for instance, that your 11-year-old is upset from fighting with her close friend. She will feel a lot better when she identifies potential ways forward, perhaps by making a conciliatory gesture to her former friend or maybe by joining a school club where she can form new relationships. The ability to navigate through difficult times is a skill that all children can learn, through parental support and everyday life experience. There is much you can do to empower your child with a more dynamic perspective on the challenges she meets throughout her day-to-day life.

Present, past and future

The ability to spot possibilities for progress and change involves three components:

Accepting the present There is no point in denying reality. A child who is struggling, say, to learn science in high school faces a real problem. Of course, you should give her words of encouragement and reassurance – that always helps – but the present problem that concerns her won't go away by burying her head in the sand. However, acceptance of the present is different from simply submitting to it. Having a positive, honest view of where she is right now helps her plan for change.

Making a list of all the possiblities in a course of action is a good way for your child to prioritize and reach a decision.

Discovery by trial and error

Stage 1: Identify Suggest to your child that she draws up a list of all the possible courses of action. Writing them down in a list and then organizing them in terms of preferences and priorities concentrates her thoughts. Chat to her about all the possible alternatives so that she has a clear idea of what is most likely to work. She will probably have to strike a balance between what she would prefer to achieve and what she can realistically expect to achieve.

Stage 2: Test out Then it is a case of testing each possibility out through the process of trial and error. Make sure that she sticks to her plan for, say, two weeks before giving up on that particular possibility – change rarely occurs quickly. Talk to her about why she thinks success eluded her on this occasion, and then work with her as she moves on to the next possibility. Eventually she will hit the mark.

Understanding the past Possibilities become more obvious to your child when she is able to learn from previous experience. That is why it is helpful to suggest that, while she is troubled by the present problem, she should focus on the previous times when she faced a similar type of difficulty and yet managed to find a way through it. The same strategies used then could be just what's required this time too.

Anticipating the future No matter how gloomy the future looks through your child's eyes, it will seem a lot brighter when she has a plan of action. Her happiness will rise when she begins to realize that she is not trapped and that she can begin to regain control of her future. It is all about forward planning,

Your child can learn how to navigate the sometimes difficult waters of childhood with your support and from experience.

in an appropriate and focused way. The more she does this, the easier it becomes.

Once the possibilities for change have been spotted – preferably through joint discussion with your child – the next stage is to implement them. Planning on its own is insufficient without actual implementation. However, there is always a risk of failure. Make it clear to your child that success isn't always guaranteed, even though that is what you all hope she will achieve. In this way, she won't stumble the moment she finds an obstacle in her way.

Problem-solving

Your child's happiness is at risk when he is faced with a difficult problem that he believes he cannot solve. You know there is a solution for every dilemma he faces, but he doesn't know that... yet. It is down to you to help hone his problem-solving skills.

The problem-solving habit

Your child improves his problem-solving skills gradually, through your guidance and through practical experience. He needs time to improve so be patient with him – what may seem to you like an obvious way out of the difficulty he faces may not even occur as a remote possibility to your child. Expect a long, slow learning curve when it comes to getting him into the habit of problem-solving.

Part of the challenge is building up his confidence to take risks, getting him to accept that sometimes his solutions won't be effective. It may help to reassure him that although his first idea didn't turn out to be useful, that doesn't mean his next solution won't be successful.

Problem-solving takes time to learn and your child may be thrown by what he sees as the hugeness of the problem.

Problem-solving **strategy**

Start by encouraging your child accurately to assess the facts of the particular problem that is troubling him, without getting tied up in associated emotions that often cloud problem-solving. Once you have heard his side of the story, get him to focus on the detail of the issue by directing specific questions at him, without talking about the emotional impact.

Ask your child to set an emotion-free target, one that he can describe in objective terms. Setting out the target so precisely will help him to focus his attention more clearly on finding solutions.

Make sure that your child has 'thinking time' to let him push the ideas and facts around in his head without any pressure to come to a conclusion. Sometimes a possible solution spontaneously emerges during this emotion-free early stage in problem-solving, even though that is not the main purpose of this stage.

After a few days, chat with your child again. This time, however, talk about any ideas he has for solving the problem. Let him express all his ideas, practical or not. Talk through each one with him. Examine the implications of each suggestion for himself, the other person or people involved and for others in the family.

How it **works** in practice

Suppose, for instance, that your nine-year-old complains to you that his older sister constantly plays with his computer without asking his permission, no matter how often he reminds her to leave his possessions alone. Ask him how often she plays with his computer without his permission. When she does do this, how long does she play with it? What program does his sister use during those periods of unauthorized access? Is there a pattern to her behaviour?

The emotion-free target could be, for example, that his sister doesn't touch his computer at all, or that she can play with it once he has given her permission to use it.

Reassure your child that he doesn't need to come up with an immediate solution – there is plenty of time. Suggest that he simply thinks about the facts of the problem for a couple of days, without specifically searching for a solution.

Your nine-year-old might suggest, for instance, that a lock is fitted to his bedroom so that his sister cannot enter uninvited. But that also affects you (you won't be able to get in without a key) and him (he will have to remember to lock and unlock it each time). Discuss all his ideas, volunteer some of your own and then finally steer him towards the one that he believes is best suited to solving the particular problem he faces.

Achievement and enjoyment

We all like success, and your child is no exception to this rule. The importance of outcome is emphasized at every stage in your child's life, especially once she starts school. Small wonder, then, that your child can become obsessed with results.

Enjoyable effort

Some children are more competitive than others, in some cases because they are self-driven and in others because their parents push them hard. Yet there is no reason why your child can't try hard at school – or at her hobbies – and be able to relax and have fun at the same time. School is not all about work and formal learning – it is also about your child having opportunities to develop her personality, friendships and interests, as well enjoying herself. Your school-age child needs your help in order to find a balance, because if over-stressed, she will inevitably become unhappy, and an unhappy child doesn't learn as well or as easily as one who is enjoying herself and is settled, confident and relaxed.

The effects of stress

The effects of stress on a child's school performance are not clear-cut. For instance, a little stress can actually be helpful – a small worry about potential failure may be just what she needs to motivate her to work harder. However, a large amount of stress can be unhelpful – too much anxiety and fear of failure can make her so psychologically overwhelmed that she gives up altogether. So when you encourage your child to put lots of effort into her school work, don't overdo the pressure or it could backfire.

Success is part of life, especially at school, but let your child know that taking part and giving his best is also important.

What you can **do**

Reinforce the point to your child that there is only one winner in a contest, and that only one child can be top of the class. Explain that this means that the ultimate prize will elude your child many times, no matter how hard she tries. Try to make her feel good about herself by emphasizing how delighted you are that she took part at all, despite the fact that she didn't achieve her target.

Help her prepare and plan in advance for whatever the competition is (whether in or out of school) – this develops her serious attitude towards achievement. By drawing her attention to the preparation, you reinforce that strategy. Recommend that she takes a forward-thinking approach to any challenge, whether that means a physical training schedule for sports day or a study schedule for up-coming school exams.

Give your child incentives to try hard, for instance, special treats or a small present. Small bonuses stimulate her desire to try. Remind her that many great achievements have been made in science, medicine and other professions only through dogged persistence. Her motivation can be maintained by your positive comments about effort rather than results, and by positive reinforcement using rewards.

When trying to ensure that your child tries hard to achieve in school, use lots of praise. For instance, give her your approval when she works furiously in preparation for a test or when she completes her homework without much prompting. Let her know that you are delighted with her effort.

What you can **say**

'I'm glad you have entered the competition, but please remember that you can't win every time. Only one child gets first prize.'

'I'm very pleased that you prepared so well. I know it wasn't easy for you and you gave up a lot of your spare time.'

'Your effort was amazing. Although you didn't win this time, you never know what can happen the next time if you put in the same effort.'

'I'm delighted that you tried so hard without me having to push you all the time. It's much better that you did this without me having to hound you.'

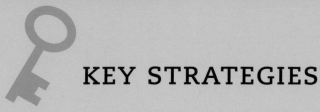

KEY STRATEGIES

Courage-boosters

Even the most courageous child can appear timid at times, depending on the context. For example, your child may be brimming with confidence when it comes to swimming in the local pool, yet he might be afraid when learning to ride a bicycle.

Dig deep

No matter how much your child trembles, always assume that deep down inside he has the courage and ability to beat the challenge in front of him, and that your job is to help him locate that inner strength. Avoid the trap of stereotyping your child as afraid, because if that is how you see him, he will never find the necessary strength to overcome what frightens him. When he lacks courage, he is heavily influenced by your expectations of him, and if you genuinely believe in him, then his own self-belief will rise. In fact, that might be just what your child needs to dig deep into his inner resources.

Going against the grain

Not following the crowd takes a special type of courage, and your child may find this extremely difficult. It is never easy for someone to take a stance that is unpopular with his peers. Therefore, try to develop his confidence in self-expression so that he is willing to express a point of view, even though it might run counter to the ideas held by his friends and others in his class. And let him know how pleased you are with him when does speak his mind in the face of peer-group opposition. Your approval strengthens his determination to develop his own opinions rather than simply following the crowd.

What you can do

Here are ten strategies to help you boost your child's courage when it appears to be flagging in the face of life's challenges:

Listen sympathetically Let your child voice his fears to you, even though they might seem silly. If you don't provide a sympathetic ear, he will worry silently and this will reduce his courage even further.

Offer understanding You will not boost your child's courage by making fun of him and his timidity. Instead, show sympathy and understanding so that he feels you are on his side. This makes him feel stronger and more able to cope.

Stress his strengths Whenever he tells you that he can't tackle a challenge because he lacks the necessary skills, point out all his other personal strengths and positive attributes, as this helps him focus on what he can do, not what he can't do.

Endorse his individuality You may be tempted to encourage him to be courageous by comparing him to other children who seem fearless. But your child will simply view himself even more negatively when compared to his peers.

O— **Put him in control** Lack of courage often stems from a perceived lack of control. That is why you should put your child back in the driving seat. Get him used to making small choices and minor decisions in his life, such as what books to read or what clothes to wear.

O— **Tackle tasks in stages** You can increase your child's courage when he faces the prospect of learning a new skill by breaking it down into small steps, each one progressing slightly further than the previous one.

O— **Choose a coaxing approach** Coercing a child into tackling something that he is afraid of rarely proves an effective courage-boosting strategy. Far better to coax and persuade until he feels more courageous than he did at the beginning.

O— **Use positive language** When persuading your timid child to try something new, talk about how much he will enjoy it, how capable he is if he would only try and how confident you are that he can do it.

O— **Be attentive** Your interest in his everyday life lifts his general level of courage. Knowing that you are a significant part of his life and that you care about him and his activities makes him feel strong.

O— **Give him praise** No matter how little he achieves, tell him how pleased you are that he made an effort. Reassure your child that the same challenge may be easier for him the next time.

Part of positive parenting is helping your child to overcome obstacles – some of which may seem enormous to him.

Feelings

What makes her tick

Your child seems so volatile at times. One minute she is sitting happily with her friends, but the next minute she explodes with rage – and you haven't a clue why she switched so quickly from one mood to another. Understanding what makes your child tick can appear an impossible task at times!

Key emotional needs

Itemized below are the four main emotional needs that drive your growing child. Your awareness that these emotional needs make your child tick doesn't mean that she is any easier to live with, but it does help you understand much of what may appear to be difficult behaviour:

1 The need to have friends From the age of four onwards, your child's desire for friends becomes a strong emotional need. It is not simply that she likes company of children her own age, it is that she needs these social relationships. By the time she is around the age of 11 or 12 years old, friendships have become the main vehicle for her to learn and develop. When she has lots of friends who are loyal and true to her, she is happy, but when she feels alone and friendless, the world seems a much sadder place to her. Guide her in peer relationships. Encourage those friendships that you think can make a positive contribution to her progress and tacitly discourage social relationships that you think aren't in her best interests.

2 The need to achieve Your child wants to succeed, but she may over-estimate her own ability. Some children think they can do anything; they have no self-doubts. The truth is, however, that every child does have limits and your child's discovery that some challenges are beyond her will diminish her confidence. That is why you should encourage her to have a realistic view of herself and her skills; optimism is psychologically healthy, but over-optimism can lead to huge disappointment and failure. Help her achieve that much-wanted success, while making sure she doesn't aim for something that is unrealistically difficult for her. Guide her as best you can towards her goal, and comfort her if she falls short of achieving it.

ABOVE LEFT AND RIGHT All children need to have friends, not only because they are fun, but increasingly, it is through friendship that your child will learn and develop.

3 The need to be loved No matter how old your child is, she continues to need your love, and she is devastated when she thinks there may be a risk that this will be withdrawn. For instance, she may push you and push you all day with her incessant demands, no matter what you say to her, without being concerned at all. Yet when you lose your temper with her, she becomes distressed and anxious because she worries that this means you don't love her any more. In time, she learns that you can love her and be annoyed with her at the same time, but in the meantime she may be rocked by your rebukes. Be prepared to reassure and console her, even though she might have been confronting you all day.

4 The need to exercise control Once your child has passed the infant stage, she increasingly likes to be in charge. She wants to be the one who decides where she can go, what she can eat and what objects she can touch, and she is not at all happy when you try to establish rules around the house. The moment you say 'no' to your child, her hackles rise because she has a psychological need to be in control. You will probably spend a lot of time explaining to her that you are the person at home who decides on the rules, not her, and that you are the person who decides what she can and cannot do at home, not her. Your child gradually learns to manage her desire to be in control.

Controlling temper

By the time your child is four or five years old, you can reasonably expect him to make more of an effort to control his anger. He now needs to be encouraged to take more responsibility for managing his rage, instead of relying on you to calm him down.

Expressing anger

Anger can be expressed in many different ways, most typically through verbal and physical violence (shouting and hitting), but there are other more subtle forms, such as insults, threatening facial expressions, close body proximity, whispering and deliberate ignoring. Much depends on your child's age and stage of development.

Gaining control

Give some practical suggestions for him to control his temper himself. For instance, he could simply come to tell you that he is beginning to feel angry, he could

Small children find it difficult to control anger. By four or five your child will begin to get to grips with this volatile emotion.

Ages and stages of anger

4–6 years Most five-year-olds have learned that physical violence is unacceptable, and while there may be occasional episodes of this, temper is usually expressed more verbally.

7–9 years As social relationships assume much greater importance now, temper is often shown through deliberate social exclusion, such as keeping the other child out of the game or keeping them off the party invitation list.

10–12 years Having reached social maturity, an angry child uses more subtle means. Spiteful behaviour – for instance, deliberately spreading false tales or teasing about appearance or attainments – is very effective and hurtful.

What to **do**

Take a preventative approach. If your child is prone to temper outbursts, talk to him about anger control when he is settled and relaxed, not when he is raging. Deflate situations before explosion point is reached, and don't let grievances fester.

Explain consequences. When discussing angry behaviour with your child, explain that you don't like it when he hits and screams, and that other children dislike it as well. Tell him that his friends will stop playing with him.

Make punishments clear. Let him know that he will be punished for uncontrolled angry outbursts, and spell out these punishments – for example, he will be sent to another room, away from the others.

Be positive. Always praise him for his positive behaviour, whenever you can. For instance, make a big fuss of him when he plays with other children without losing his temper, even though he has been provoked.

walk away from the troubling situation or he could watch his favourite DVD. In addition, suggest that he voices anger instead of acting on it. Explain that it is better for him to say, 'I'm getting angry because I can't finish my homework', than it is for him to say nothing, become increasingly cross and then to throw the books on the floor in temper.

Make a list of all these possibilities, and ask your child for some suggestions as well, then decide in

What **not** to do

Don't force an apology. Rather than attempt to make your child apologize for an outburst of temper, which is likely to end in failure anyway, you can still try to encourage him to say sorry. This helps him recognize that this form of anger is unacceptable.

Don't treat any incidents lightly. Remember that the victim of your child's temper has suffered as a result, so don't dismiss those episodes as trivial – they are very real to whoever is on the receiving end.

Never match anger with anger. The suggestion, for instance, that a parent should rage at their child in retaliation for his rage is counter-productive. That sort of behaviour sets a highly undesirable example for the child to copy.

Don't drag out each episode. Once he has calmed down and you have sorted out the problem, be prepared to move on. Continuing to discuss what happened previously will eventually become counter-productive.

consultation with him what methods he should use whenever he starts to feel angry. Practise these strategies with your child in a role-play situation so that he knows what to do when the real situation occurs. Gaining temper control usually takes time, so try not to expect sudden improvements. With your encouragement and support, however, he will get there eventually and both you and your child will notice the difference.

Personal space

Your child's desire for privacy begins to emerge from the age of eight or nine. Whereas before he was probably very happy to share everything with you, now he begins to keep things to himself. His need for personal space increases as he gets older.

This is mine!

Personal ownership matters to him. For instance, he likes to have his own room, his own computer and to be able to play unsupervised when his friends come over. This is also the age when he starts to complain vociferously (if he hasn't done so before) because his younger siblings keep touching his toys and possessions – he wants his own personal space at home, and this is one of the keys to his happiness. So don't look on this as a sign of rejection; instead, look on it as a sign of healthy psychological development.

Keeping himself to himself

Explain to him that you respect his right to privacy, and that you understand his need for personal space. In the same way that you are entitled to have inner thoughts that you keep to yourself, he is also entitled to the same. Add, however, that it is always good for a child to share his worries, concerns and ideas with his parents because they are able to guide and support him. Remind him that you can help him find a solution to any difficulty he faces and that discussing ideas and emotions with you will help him understand them better. Through experience and from your advice, your child steadily learns how to find a suitable balance between sharing everything he has with others and keeping everything private.

How to provide personal space

The following are some suggestions to help you give your child the personal space he needs:

♡ **Let go** You may have difficulty letting go a little at this stage in your child's life. After all, you are used to him spontaneously sharing his stories, his excitements and his ideas with you, and you want that closeness to continue. This is a new phase for you, and you could have a sense that your 'little one' is changing before your eyes.

♡ **Be open with him** Chat to him about your concerns. Explain to your child that you recognize his need for a little more personal space now that he is older, but at the same time make sure he understands that he can be open with you and yet have privacy at the same time. Help him find that balance.

♡ **Establish guidelines** Don't leave everything to chance, however. Agree on clear guidelines about the extent of his personal space and privacy. For example, maybe he can use the internet in his room on his own, but he can only go to websites that you have previously approved. Your trust in him will encourage him to be responsive to you. Clear guidelines are useful for both of you.

As children get older, their need for private space increases; sometimes parents find this issue a difficult one to negotiate.

♡ **Protect his privacy** Make sure that the others in the family also respect his privacy, especially his siblings. Tell them, for instance, that they are to knock before entering his room and to keep out unless he personally invites them in. Your child will feel very mature and important when he hears you set out these rules to his brothers and sisters.

♡ **Make him feel responsible** In your discussions with him, add that he has a responsibility to prove to you that he is capable of managing this privacy, this increased personal space. Explain that he shouldn't get up to mischief when he is on his own, and that he shouldn't do anything that you would disapprove of or be upset about.

Internet use

Your child won't want you looking over his shoulder when he is chatting with someone on the internet, or texting on his mobile, and that is probably a reasonable request from a child aged 11 or 12 years. However, make sure that you lay down the ground rules for web language and behaviour, such as no swearing or abusive language. Talk about internet safety issues, such as never giving his personal details in a chat room and never arranging to meet someone he has met virtually on the internet. Seek assurances from your child that he will always observe and abide by these rules.

Jealousy

Jealousy is one of the more unpleasant human characteristics. It is a mixture of resentment, fear, insecurity, possessiveness and suspicion – not the sort of emotions we readily admit to. Yet jealousy is probably a feeling that we all experience at one time or another.

Impact

At best, jealousy makes your child very unhappy and dissatisfied, and at worst it sends him into a foul mood that results in him carrying out hurtful actions against others. Your child can be jealous of his siblings or his peers, when he thinks he is being treated less favourably than them. He can also be jealous about possessions, either hoarding his own or wanting what another child has. He may also be jealous when he sees you giving your attention to another child within your family.

Sibling rivalry

The most common form of jealousy in childhood is sibling rivalry, that is, resentment against brothers or sisters, and this is so common in virtually every family that most psychologists now regard it as normal. You can rest assured that your children are not the only ones to fight with each other! Sibling rivalry occurs because parents have a limited amount of time, attention and resources, and the more children there are in a family, the less there is to go round. It is hardly surprising, therefore, that at times your children feel that their siblings are rivals.

Yet the intensity of sibling rivalry varies from family to family, and even within the same family. The age gap between the children makes a difference. An age gap of around two years is usually associated with strong jealousy between siblings, probably because they each feel threatened by the other. With a large age gap, the children have quite different interests, and with a very small age gap, the children are likely to share the same interests. Sibling jealousy typically starts when the first-born resents the arrival of his younger brother or sister. He may feel that you don't love him as much, or that you prefer the new baby. He needs to feel that you think he is special too. Fortunately there is a lot you can do to make sibling rivalry less likely to occur in your family, although some instances of bickering amongst your children are probably inevitable.

Sibling rivalry is a normal part of family life – try to spend time with each child to prevent anyone feeling shortchanged.

What you can **do**

Although you may feel annoyed at your child's jealousy, don't make him feel guilty. If you do confront him in a challenging way, he will simply keep his thoughts and ideas to himself. He will also begin to see himself in negative terms.

Let your child know that you understand what it is like to be jealous of someone else. There is no harm in admitting to him that you also feel jealous at times, as long as you add that you don't let these feelings upset you, overcome you or spoil your enjoyment of anything.

Emphasize the positives. His jealousy is based on a perceived advantage that his friend has – for instance, better clothes or better exam results – and you can help by focusing your child's attention on his own strengths.

If your children show signs of sibling rivalry, aim for fairness, not equality. Each child is an individual, with his own particular emotional needs, and each of your children needs love and attention in varying amounts and in different ways.

What you can **say**

'I can see you that you're jealous of your sister, and I'm glad that you have told me about it instead of bottling it up. I'm sure you'll feel better once we've had a chat about what's troubling you.'

'I totally understand what you're feeling right now. Sometimes I get jealous too, but I don't let these feelings grab hold of me. I find that resentment tends to go away after a while, and that will happen to you as well.'

'I can see that you're feeling bad because your friend has more money to spend than you and has the latest clothes. But you have plenty of things as well. Try to look at all the things you've got instead of all the things your friend has.'

'You're different from your sister, so I prefer to give you what you especially want, rather than giving you and your sister exactly the same. So by treating both of you differently, you each get what you really want or need.'

Shyness

Every child can suddenly become shy, depending on the circumstances. You may be surprised to see your confident child – who is normally friendly and full of conversation – become withdrawn and uncomfortable in some social situations with other children and adults.

Shyness trends

Research shows that more than 80 per cent of all adults consider that they were shy at least once during their childhood. When asked to classify their child in terms of their sociability, over one-third of all parents described them as shy. Over 40 per cent of children aged between four and 12 years rate themselves as shy. There is evidence that a child is more likely to be shy in an environment that values competitiveness and attainments, rather than valuing a child for her personal qualities. Before the age of five years, boys tend to have a higher level of shyness than girls, but this trend reverses once the children attend school. Between 25 and 50 per cent of shy children are reported to have nightmares, while less than 10 per cent of non-shy children have nightmares.

Where shyness comes from

Although there is no single source of shyness, there does seem to be a family connection. Put simply, shy parents tend to have shy children. One explanation for this finding is that shyness is genetically inherited from parents, just as other characteristics are inherited, and there is some scientific evidence to support this view. However, another explanation is that when parents are shy themselves, the model of social behaviour experienced at home – which the children will naturally copy – is one of shyness, and therefore the children themselves are more likely to be shy. The chances are that there is some truth in both explanations.

LEFT AND BELOW More than 80 per cent of adults think that they were shy at some point in their childhood and it seems that shy parents make for shy children.

Q When my child becomes shy, I am tempted to cajole her out of it. Sometimes this works. Is this the best approach?

A While this method can be effective, it can also be counter-productive – your child could just retreat into herself even more. A far better approach is to acknowledge her feelings. She may be afraid that you will laugh at her social anxiety, so talk to her about her shyness, as that will bring the subject into the open. Let her know that you understand about shyness, that you have been shy too and that it's okay to be shy sometimes. Tell her that you care for her even when she is shy, but that you are sure she would have more fun if she spoke to others. Reassure her that other children are like her. Once your child knows that you understand what she is feeling, she is more likely to be comfortable and cooperate with any plan for change and progress.

Q Can a child overcome her shyness?

A Of course she can, when she is given the right sort of support. There's no point in simply insisting that she becomes talkative. Instead, set an attainable goal, such as just saying hello to another child – she is more likely to experience success this way. And don't make her the centre of attention; a shy child hates when everyone stares at her, so avoid this if at all possible. For instance, when in a group, she should not be asked to sing in front of the others or to tell her latest news. In practical terms, discourage 'shy' behaviour that makes her look socially awkward, for example, looking down at her feet or sucking her thumb.

Motivation

Everybody loves a winner. But everyone also loves a child who is so motivated that she tries as hard as she can, even if she doesn't succeed all the time. There is nothing quite like watching your child determinedly struggle against the odds in order to achieve a goal.

When she couldn't care less

It is troubling when her motivation is low and she displays a couldn't-care-less attitude. Look for reasons why this has happened, rather than simply assuming that she is bored and needs a change. Maybe her motivation has dropped because she never really wanted to take part in the activity in the first place. Perhaps she dislikes her teacher, or it could be that the teaching methods don't suit her. There is also the possibility that she is just trying to cram too much into her week and her psychological energy levels are running out.

Motivating a child to give his or her best is important, but sympathizing with the difficult bits is also key.

What you **can** say

'I'm pleased that you tried so hard.' Recognition of your child's effort in trying to complete a difficult challenge makes her feel valued. Your acknowledgement that she tried hard raises her motivation and is enough to make her try hard the next time as well.

'I can see this is difficult for you.' It is always helpful to show your child that you realize life can be difficult for her at times. Your empathy, rather than criticism or ridicule, stimulates her motivation because she feels that you support her and that you don't blame her.

'There were times when I found things boring at your age.' It is normal for a child occasionally to have fluctuating interest in activities. By pointing out that your interest varied too at that age, your child begins to believe this will be a temporary phase that should soon pass.

'Let's think of ways we could make this more interesting for you.' Ask your child to think about possible changes to make the activity or challenge more attractive. Perhaps she would like to change her seating in class, or to attend a new after-school club. Basic changes could be helpful.

'I'm so proud of you.' There is no better boost to motivation than praise. It doesn't matter that your child took all week, for example, to finish her maths assignment while her friend completed it in half the time – she deserves your praise and approval.

What **not** to say

'You should be able to do that because it's easy.' The challenge may seem easy from your point of view, but if your child's motivation is wavering, then it is probably not easy for her. Your suggestion reduces her enthusiasm even further by making her feel stupid and inadequate.

'You just need to try harder.' Don't assume that your child's lack of motivation is due to lack of effort. In many instances, a child's slump in enthusiasm arises because she struggles despite all her effort, not because she doesn't try.

'You should be more interested in that.' The chances are that she would like to be more interested, but that for some reason – which she probably doesn't understand – motivation eludes her. A stern admonition is unlikely to raise her motivation.

'I don't know why you dislike this; I loved it at your age.' Your child is a unique individual with her own interests, likes and dislikes. Her tastes don't always match yours. Although you want to stimulate her motivation, this particular comment could have the opposite effect.

'I'm so disappointed that you didn't come first.' In every class test, in every race, only one child can come first. By all means have high aspirations for your child, but don't make her feel a failure because she missed first place. At least she tried.

Positive discipline

The essence of positive discipline is that it emphasizes what a child does right more than what he does wrong, and uses rewards more than punishments. It is a much more enjoyable approach for you and your child than a negative one, and you will both be happier and the atmosphere at home will be more relaxed.

The art of gentle criticism

There is nothing wrong with discipline. In fact, without rules and guidance about his behaviour, his happiness would soon drop because he won't know what to expect or what to do. A consistent, structured discipline makes him feel contented, safe and secure.

The art of delivering gentle criticism involves a very careful and positive use of language. Instead of complaining about actions that you disapprove of, place your comments in the context of his favourable characteristics, for instance, 'I'm astonished at how angry you are with your sister because you're usually such a happy and pleasant child.' Your child may react more agreeably to this approach. Try to phrase criticism so that you criticize your child's behaviour, not your child himself. Suppose your child has told you that he has completed his homework, but you discover that he hasn't even started it. A positive-discipline approach would be to say, 'I don't like it when you hide things from me' (criticizing his behaviour), instead of saying, 'You're horrible when you tell me lies' (criticizing your child). This approach avoids unnecessary confrontation between you and your child, while still enabling you to get your message across to him. And that more positive outcome makes you both feel better.

Positive-discipline techniques

Follow these strategies to help you establish discipline in a non-combative way:

♡ **Highlight examples of good behaviour** Instead of solely reprimanding your child when he misbehaves, give him lots of praise when he does behave appropriately. Tell him, for example, that you were delighted by the way he helped you with the household chores. Your child thrives under your approval and praise.

♡ **Find positives every day** No matter how trying a day you have had due to confrontations with your child, find something about his behaviour that you can praise. Sometimes you might have to dig deep to find an instance that merits your enthusiasm, but do it anyway! Aim to end each day on a positive note.

♡ **Reject smacking** Part of positive discipline is a commitment that you won't smack your child. Physical violence (and that is what a smack is, no matter how innocently you describe it) hurts your child, makes him afraid and reduces his feeling of security with you. And what's more, smacking doesn't have any long-term remedial effect.

♡ Use more rewards than punishments If you spend more time punishing your child for misbehaviour than rewarding him for his good behaviour, then maybe it is time to rethink your approach. Perhaps you can ignore some of the minor infractions and be more sensitive to the positive moments.

♡ Frame rules positively Rules about behaviour usually fall into two categories: those that start with 'do' and those that start with 'don't'. In most cases, a 'don't' rule can be reframed positively. For example, 'Don't be late home from football practice' can be rephrased as 'Please come home from football practice in time'.

♡ Use criticism sparingly Regularly criticizing your child for his misbehaviour is unlikely to have any positive effect in the short term, and in the long term

it will make him very unhappy. There is a place for criticism in family life – nobody is perfect all the time – but too much of it can create tension between you and your child.

♡ Express positive feelings No matter how much you feel provoked by your child's challenging behaviour, make sure you tell him regularly that you love him. He needs to hear these words from you, no matter what sort of day you have had with each other. Unconditional love should underpin all discipline with your child.

Rules are part of discipline and your child needs to know what they are, but also be positive and give praise for good behaviour.

Heart or head

Children need to learn to plan ahead to make appropriate decisions, and this is rarely a skill that develops spontaneously. The ability to forward-plan usually increases a child's success, and allows her to structure her time and effort more effectively. There are children who are naturally reflective and cautious, while others tend to act impulsively.

With or without a plan

Some children plan ahead and make a decision only after they have thought long and hard about the problem facing them, having weighed up the advantages and disadvantages very carefully until they are absolutely certain that this is the right way forward. These children lead with their head, make advanced plans and think before they act. Others, however, make decisions instantly, without spending much time planning ahead or considering the implications of their choice. It is the first feeling that counts for these children; their response is emotional, not rational. They lead with their heart and act without forward-planning.

Contrasting characteristics

Children can be divided into two groups when it comes to tackling a problem or making a decision:

Reflective

The reflective child likes to take an overview before making up her mind. She is not cold and methodical; she simply prefers to have all the facts to help her plan ahead. She thinks deeply about things, examining the alternatives in great detail before committing herself to a course of action. The reflective child is more likely to let her head rule over her heart when decision-making.

Impulsive

The impulsive child likes to reach a decision almost instantly, without a planning strategy. Her reluctance to consider the pros and cons is not laziness – she just prefers to get the matter over and done with. She acts quickly, whether it is deciding what snack to have in school that morning or who to invite to her birthday party. The impulsive child lets her heart rule over her head. Plans aren't of interest to her.

Research findings

Research has shown that these characteristics tend to be very stable during childhood, which means that a child who is reflective at the age of five or six years is likely to be reflective when she is older, and the same applies to the impulsive child.

An impulsive child typically makes more mistakes than the one who pauses before acting, because she makes her choice so quickly; the reflective child, on the other hand, makes wrong choices less frequently. Yet some decisions have to be made instantly. For instance, a child who is halfway across the road and sees a car fast approaching must reach the pavement as quickly as she can. She doesn't have time to consider whether it is a car or a bus that is coming and whether she should retrace her steps or cross to the other side – all that matters is to reach the safety zone as speedily as possible.

From heart to head

Encourage her to take more time than usual before making up her mind.

Suggest that she considers her decision a couple of times before acting on it.

Point out how every decision she needs to make has more than one possible outcome.

Praise her when she does take a little more time than usual to reach an answer.

Give her an example that shows how you reached a decision reflectively.

From head to heart

Try to give her enough confidence so that she becomes more decisive.

Encourage her to follow through with her plan as soon as she makes up her mind.

Persuade her to make broad decisions without focusing on small details.

Give her lots of approval when she acts decisively and confidently.

Give her an example that shows you can make your mind up very quickly.

Nuturing change

If your child is ruled by her heart and you think that she might benefit from listening to her head a little, you can help her to become more reflective. Conversely, if your child is ruled by her head and you think that it might be helpful if she listened to her heart to some extent, you can encourage her to become more impulsive. The chart above offers some suggestions on how to achieve this change.

However, expect some resistance. Your child uses a style of decision-making that suits her personality and thinking skills. Therefore she may hold on to her current planning style quite tenaciously.

Forward planning is a skill that parents can help foster; for a child anxious about change, this can make life less frightening.

Emotional resilience

Your child's ability to bounce back from the ups and downs of everyday life has a huge influence on his level of happiness. It is amazing how some children cope easily with the rough-and-tumble of life, are immune to teasing from others and appear resistant to upsets.

Resilience factors

Psychologists don't know for sure why one child is more easily upset than others or why one is more resilient to stress than others. Certainly, you only need to watch a group of children interact to see that some seem to be happy without a care in the world, while others burst into tears or sink into a bad mood with hardly any provocation at all. Some are able to maintain a high level of self-confidence even in the face of minor failures. Others, however, seem to crumble psychologically the moment something goes wrong. If your child lacks emotional resilience, you will spend much of the time drying his tears and reassuring him that the world is not such a bad place after all. There are a number of factors that probably play a part in developing your child's emotional resilience, including inherited characteristics, previous experience, upbringing and temperament. A lack of emotional resilience leads to unhappiness, weak self-esteem and higher levels of anxiety.

Home dimensions

A child's emotional resilience is more likely to develop in a family that:

- Has a clear and consistent discipline that the children are expected to follow.
- Accepts that mistakes and failure are part of the learning process.
- Encourages open discussion of feelings, aspirations and worries.
- Helps children develop empathy and understanding of other people's feelings.
- Provides the children with demanding – but manageable – challenges.
- Expects children to be independent, and to manage without constantly asking for help.
- Welcomes initiative, even if the idea turns out to be less successful than anticipated.

Some children burst into tears at the first sign of adversity while others seem able to ride the storms of childhood.

What you can do

Encouraging your child to think about incidents that upset him previously, such as teasing from another child in pre-school, will help him to understand and develop from his experiences. In this way, he can learn from the past.

Listening to his anxieties, such as being afraid to go to the party because he was worried that others might ignore him, will show him that you take him seriously and will help rebuild his self-esteem.

If your child spends too much time worrying about what he thinks he can't do, he soon forgets about all the things he can do. This soon develops into a negative spiral in which his confidence tumbles lower and lower.

Self-doubts make him think negatively when he faces a new challenge – for instance, he expects to fail or assumes that he won't be as well liked as the others. Encourage him to think positively. Your child thrives under your attention and interest, and he will be much less affected by the knocks of everyday life when he feels loved, valued and special. Your belief in him strengthens his self-belief.

Rather than focusing inwards on himself, encourage him in the habit of caring for others. This often has the effect of strengthening emotional resilience. Although he might grumble, it will eventually make him feel better about himself.

How you can do it

Talk to him about the reasons why he needs so much reassurance, and suggest alternative ways in which he could respond. For example, instead of crying, suggest that he says, 'I don't care what you say.'

Ask him to explain to you what he is afraid of and let him see that you understand his concerns. Then give him plenty of reassurance and, where possible, suggest basic coping strategies, such as smiling even when he is nervous and making good eye contact.

Shift his focus on to his abilities, not his deficits, by pointing out all his good points. Remind him of his previous achievements, and reassure him that he is just as capable now as he was then.

Encourage your child to have positive thoughts by saying to himself, for instance, 'I can do this well' or 'The children will like me'. Known as 'positive self-talk', this form of inner language can significantly lift his self-confidence.

Take the opportunity every day to let him know that you think he is great and that you believe in him. Don't hesitate to make these positive comments – he may shrug his shoulders nonchalantly, but he will love every word of it!

Common challenges

Every child experiences problems outside their – and your – control at some stage, and no matter how capable and confident your child is, at these times anxiety takes over and her happiness ebbs away. There are several ways in which you can help her to face up to and cope with these common challenges, and regain her emotional equilibrium.

I don't like school

Suppose your child tells you that she doesn't like school any more and that she doesn't want to go back there. You can see that she is unhappy, but she doesn't know what to do to make things better. Help her reach a solution. Firstly, give her a chance to explain her concerns. Make it clear to her that you care and that you will help her, but also make it clear that she has to attend school while you sort things out. Perhaps she has difficulties in the playground or maybe the work is too demanding for her. Secondly, speak to her teachers and try to institute some change that will make the situation better for her – a change of school is rarely the answer.

Family break-up

This is another childhood challenge that an increasing number of children have to deal with. But it can be managed effectively so that she comes through relatively unscathed emotionally. There is no doubt, of course, that a child will be dreadfully upset when she learns about the split – she will be tearful and angry with both parents. However, research confirms that the biggest single factor in helping children through the emotional stress of parental break-up is maintaining contact with the non-custodial parent. So even if the parents are not on especially good terms, they should make sure that their child has regular contact with both of them. It is vital that the adults don't use the children as a way of hitting back at each other.

Coping and support strategies

No matter what the problem is – your child's unhappiness at moving house, arguments with her brother or sister or a family bereavement – here are some suggestions for ways you can help her cope more effectively when things go wrong:

♡ **Tackle the problem head on** Problems are more easily resolved when they are acknowledged and tackled openly. Pretending that a difficulty doesn't exist in the hope that it will go away rarely works. Try to create a family ethos in which your children feel natural about discussing difficulties that they face.

♡ **Manage upcoming change** If you know that there is a significant change coming up in your child's life, let her know in plenty of time. For instance, when she has to move to a new school, ensure that she visits the school – and possibly even attends there for a couple of days – before the actual starting date.

♡ **Look for the upsides** Encourage your child to use the positives of the situation to support her through the challenge. If, for example, she is unhappy about moving house because she won't be able to see her friends, set a date for her old friends to come and visit her in your new house.

♡ **Answer any questions** Children have the ability to pose very difficult questions, especially when they are under pressure. A child who, for instance, is grieving for a grandparent may raise key issues about life and death; answer these as best you can. Her questions help her regain control over her feelings.

♡ **Help to find the right solutions** There is always a solution for every difficulty she faces – she just has to find it, often with your help and support. Encourage your child to think for herself and to make choices that suit her and her abilities. But if she can't identify any herself, offer possible alternative ways forward for her.

Breaking bad news

The chances are that your child will have a happy childhood. Through circumstances, however, you may find that you have to break bad news to her at some point, perhaps because a family member is seriously ill, or because your family has a financial problem or possibly because of marriage break-up. The information is easier for your child to accept if it is pitched at a level she understands – how you would speak to a four-year-old is different from what you would say to a 12-year-old. However, honesty is better than concealment, so tell her the truth. Try to explain it in a way that makes your child feel that her life will carry on much as before. And if you can see any positives in the situation, highlight them for her.

Expect lots of questions, which you should answer as openly and clearly as you can. Her reaction to hearing bad news will be heavily influenced by the way you deliver the message and by the response you give to her requests for more details.

Sometimes your child may have to be told bad news and it is better to be honest than to attempt to conceal it.

Reaching puberty

Puberty is the phase of physical and psychological growth that signals the end of childhood, as your pre-teenager's body begins to take on adult shape, size and sexual potential. Statistics confirm that the onset of puberty usually takes place between the age of nine and 14 years.

Adolescent myth

It is simply not true that adolescents are always unhappy and difficult to live with. Each child develops during puberty in his own unique way; confrontation and conflict is not inevitable. Statistics confirms that less than one in five families report serious conflict between parents and their adolescent offspring. Most conflicts at this stage consist only of minor bickering over issues such as clothes, hairstyles and responsibility for family chores; encouragingly, most adolescents are reasonably calm, cooperative and communicative with their parents, and they are predictable for much of the time. The best help you can give your child during puberty is to be sensitive to his changing needs. Take his concerns seriously, recognize that he is growing older and is capable of handling greater freedom and responsibility and be there to support him when he needs advice. With your help, there is no reason why puberty cannot be a happy period in his life.

Changes brought on by puberty

Physical There is a rapid increase in weight and height caused by an increase of hormones in the bloodstream (testosterone in boys and oestrogen in girls). This happens months in advance of any outward signs of puberty. Physical changes don't always occur smoothly and in harmony, and your child may be unhappy about the way his body shape alters.

Sexual The sex organs become larger in boys and girls, so that by the time puberty has ended, their bodies are capable of reproduction. If you have a daughter, the one event that signals her fertility is her first period; if you have a boy, then the equivalent sign of sexual maturation is ejaculation, that is, the discharge of fluid containing sperm.

Social Your child's peer group assumes greater importance in his life, and he begins to form attitudes that are the same as others his own age. In other words, peer pressure comes into play – he wants to be like his friends, to wear the same clothes as them and to listen to the same music. Peer pressure is so strong in some cases that your child may become afraid to go against anything the group suggests.

Adolescence doesn't have to be a time of conflict – 80 per cent of families report no serious difficulties with their teenagers.

Q What will the impact be if my child reaches puberty earlier or later than his friends and classmates?

A Life can be difficult for a child whose growth spurt is either ahead of his peers (when they might make fun of him for being so tall and thin) or behind his peers (when they might make fun of him for being so small). Physical appearance assumes great importance for adolescents, and any hint that they are different from their friends can be a powerful source of unhappiness. Research shows that a girl who starts puberty significantly early or late, and who therefore develops sexual characteristics at a different time from most of her peers, tends to be disadvantaged psychologically. Because she is different from her friends in school, she may be teased by them. She needs plenty of reassurance from her parents that she is not odd.

Q My child is 11 years old and is overweight. Should we put him on a diet?

A Weight control is important at this age, but formal diets are best avoided at first. Instead, a more helpful strategy would be to encourage your child to follow a healthy lifestyle that balances good nutrition (lots of fruit and vegetables, and medium-sized portions) with plenty of exercise. Think about the meals you make for him, get advice on healthy food products from your family doctor and direct your child towards physical activities such as sports, training in the gym or simply walking more than he does at present.

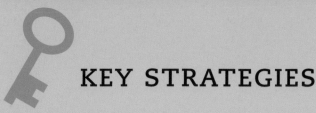

KEY STRATEGIES

Beating the blues

There are bound to be unhappy incidents that threaten your child's happiness every now and again, whether they are related to friends, family, school or clothes. It is at these times when you may have to step in and help your child beat the blues.

Talk to her

While there are many different strategies to bring your child out of a dark mood, the one technique that underpins all of them is good communication. A child who is locked into her own world of sadness – whatever the trigger for this emotional downturn might have been – is unlikely to lift herself out of it. She has negative feelings that won't go away if they are just ignored, which is why you need to talk to her. Encourage her to verbalize her feelings. At that stage, you don't even need to home in on the precise cause – you only need to get her to bring her emotions out into the open. That is half the battle, maybe more, in restoring her happiness.

What you can do

Follow these seven strategies in order to help lift your child out of a low emotional state:

O⊷ Encourage remedial action No matter what problem faces your child, encourage her to think of something she can do to make things better for herself. For instance, if she feels down because she hasn't got the right clothes, help her choose new ones that she will feel comfortable wearing. In a sense, it doesn't matter what she actually decides to do, as long as she chooses a definite course of action.

O⊷ Persuade her to own up A child can feel miserable because she knows she has done something wrong, but is afraid to confess. Guilt can be overwhelming, and the only solution is to admit to what she has done. That is never easy. Explain to your child that telling the truth about what has happened is always better than deliberately lying in order to conceal it. She will be happier when she is truthful and honest with you.

O⊷ Help maintain her routine One effect of the blues is your child's loss of interest in her normal routine. She doesn't want to do her homework, meet up with her friends or attend her music class in the evening. Don't give in to this. Instead, make sure that she sticks to her normal routine, whether she likes it or not. Routine creates stability and predictability in her world, which will help her regain her happiness.

O⊷ Suggest physical exercise Psychologists have found a link between physical exercise and psychological well-being. Going on a run, exercising in the gym or taking part in athletics won't shift the blues by itself, but it will certainly help. Unhappiness causes your child to feel lethargic and apathetic – she would rather sit in a chair and feel sorry for herself –

so encourage her to develop a routine of physical exercise and stick to it.

O—⊷ Focus on a healthy diet Common sense tells you that healthy eating is an important contributing factor to your child's development – we are what we eat! That is why you and your child should look closely at her eating habits and her daily food intake. However, be very careful not to overdo it – the pressure to diet in order to achieve a slim figure can be taken to extremes by a vulnerable teenager, perhaps resulting in anorexia.

O—⊷ Maintain good sleeping habits The blues cause your child to feel tired, and yet she complains that when she does go to bed she doesn't sleep well. So she struggles to get up in time for school, then wants to lie in bed most of the day at the weekends and during holidays. Do your best to help your child stick to normal bedtime and getting up times, even if she says she doesn't sleep well.

Childhood depression

While every child has episodes of sadness, these are typically temporary. In rare instances, however, the feeling of sadness is so intense and so long-lasting that it becomes depression. Signs of childhood depression vary, but can include withdrawal from everyday life, a sense of detachment from the world outside, apathy and lethargy, lack of interest, headaches, sore stomach and tiredness. Diagnosing depression in childhood can only be achieved by qualified mental health professionals, but if you are at all in doubt about your child's emotional well-being, consult your family doctor.

O—⊷ Think positively together There is a danger that your child's unhappiness creates such anxiety for you that you both end up feeling miserable, and that is definitely not productive. Force yourself to take a positive view, to remind yourself that this is a temporary blip that she can come through. Likewise, encourage her to have an optimistic attitude, and discourage negative statements. Help her beat the blues by working together.

A healthy diet, sufficient sleep, physical exercise and a positive approach can all help your child weather unhappy times.

Getting along with others

Kindness

It helps to remember that all children are innately caring and thoughtful. Therefore, when it comes to nurturing kindness and compassion, it is primarily a case of finding ways in which to harness and direct your child's natural inclinations.

Two dimensions of caring

There are two different aspects to caring, and you can encourage your child to engage in both (see chart opposite):

Feelings Before your child acts kindly towards others, he has to feel caring towards them. Empathy is your child's ability to experience the emotions of another person – to feel what they feel – and empathy underlies most gestures of kindness. There is some evidence that empathy is instinctive; for example, a baby cries loudly when he hears another baby cry (more so than in response to a computer-generated cry), suggesting that he is unhappy with someone else's distress; a toddler cries when he sees his parent cry; and an older child offers comfort to an unhappy friend. These pro-social actions usually occur naturally, without prompting. However, there is no harm in developing your child's empathy for others. Sympathy – that is, genuine concern for someone else's difficulties without actually understanding what the person feels – is also an important part of caring for others.

Actions Kindness also involves your child doing something for others that he doesn't actually need to do, whether that is cooperating with them, sharing with them, helping them to solve their problems or making a personal sacrifice for them. When your ten-year-old gives up his seat on the bus so that an elderly lady can sit down, you should be pleased with this very clear demonstration of a caring attitude. There are many ways in which he can demonstrate his caring attitude towards others. Kind actions can be specific to individuals (for instance, he does something to help one person) or they can be group-based (for example, he gives part of his pocket money to a charity that helps a lot of people). There are opportunities every day for your child to be kind, and the more he responds in this way, the more likely this will become second nature to him.

A small pet to care for can help foster your child's natural feelings of kindness and also encourages responsibility for others.

What you can do

Praise your child when he shows consideration towards other children and adults.

Buy him a pet to look after, if you think you can make sure that it doesn't get neglected.

Emphasize to your child that his behaviour has consequences.

Provide opportunities for your child to be helpful. Ask your child to give an example and teach sharing skills to another child.

Step in quickly if you see him behaving in an uncaring way.

Encourage your child to imagine how the other child feels as a result of his behaviour.

How you can do it

Tell him how pleased you are that he comforted his friend when he hurt his knee while playing together, or give him a special treat of an additional five minutes watching television because he helped his sister clear up her room.

Even the very basic responsibility of feeding a small domestic pet such as a fish or a hamster teaches a child that he should care for others. Supervise the arrangements so that your child actually does what is necessary to care for the pet.

Tell your child clearly, 'When you ignore me, I feel upset'. That is better than just telling him, 'Don't ignore me when I talk to you'. The more he understands the practical consequences of his behaviour, the more he will think before he acts.

Give him responsible tasks, such as setting the cutlery out for the evening meal, and persuade him to leave things nicely for other people. Small household chores develop his caring side.

Suggest to him that that he teaches his younger sibling or younger cousin how to share and to explain why sharing is good for everyone. This helps develop his own understanding of the importance of sharing.

Encourage him to think about the feelings of the recipient of his unkind act. Once his empathy for the victim is stimulated, he will start to reflect on the impact of what he has done.

Family

The key source of your child's happiness lies in her family relationships. It is her emotional connections with you and your partner, her brothers and sisters, her cousins, aunts and uncles and with close family friends that go a long way towards making her the uniquely wonderful individual that she has become.

Loving management

Positive family relationships meet her core psychological needs to be loved, to be valued and to feel safe and secure. That is how she thrives. Your child's happiness is closely linked to the emotional nourishment she receives at home. Psychologists studying family dynamics have identified two dimensions of parenting:

Warm / hostile A 'warm' parent is accepting, affectionate, uses praise and rarely punishes, while a 'hostile' parent frequently rejects their child, uses negative language and often punishes.

Restrictive / permissive A 'restrictive' parent enforces fixed rules, picks up on all misbehaviour

and discourages independent judgement, while a 'permissive' parent avoids rules, never punishes and allows complete freedom.

Evidence from research suggests that family relationships are most conducive to a child's emotional well-being when parents have a warm style that is closer to permissive than restrictive; a child raised in that system is more likely to be happy, confident, outgoing, sociable and independent.

Helping siblings to be friends

It is important to try not to intervene too soon when your children have a minor squabble. Ignoring these small disagreements may end their little quarrel more quickly than rewarding their disagreement with your attention. However, if you detect serious sibling tension, don't let it persist. If your children can't sort out their differences by themselves, get involved. Bring their complaints out into the open and suggest solutions to make the situation better for them. Try to encourage cooperation by giving your children a joint activity, such as putting away the groceries or tidying a cupboard, so that they have to work together to complete the task. Supervise these activities to ensure that they work in unison.

Making comparisons between siblings is guaranteed to cause tension between them, so no matter what the situation, avoid falling into that particular trap. Each of your children is unique and will make their own way in the world. Encourage each child to develop their individual strengths and interests, rather than to follow in each other's footsteps.

Family parties that span the generations give your child opportunities to learn the value of extended family relationships.

Q One of my children is more troublesome than the other and I'm always telling her off. It makes me feel bad and I'm worried that she'll be damaged because I appear to favour her brother.

A Favouritism inevitably has a negative effect on family relationships, no matter what the underlying reasons. Your rejected child feels alone and isolated, and your star child may feel embarrassed and responsible for his sister's unhappiness. That's why it is always best to avoid showing favouritism. If you can't stop yourself feeling more negative towards your challenging child, make a huge effort to ensure that this imbalance of feelings doesn't come through in your parenting. You may find that any tendency towards favouritism passes when you compel yourself to spend more time with her, as she could be misbehaving and acting up just to get your attention

Q How much do my child's relationships with others, such as her teachers and after-school carers, contribute to her happiness and emotional development?

A Every relationship in your child's life plays a part in her progress and psychological growth – your child is capable of forming a positive emotional connection with more than one person. Of course, most of these other social attachments are secondary to the impact of your own relationship with her, but they still have some influence all the same. Don't look on these as a threat; instead, regard them as opportunities for your child to experience different types of relationships. Each relationship complements the other.

POSITIVE PARENTING

Parents as role models

What you do as a parent affects your child's development in so many ways. But it is not just that your parenting strategies are influential, it is also that your behaviour serves as a role model for him – in many instances, he uses you as an example of how he himself should behave.

Self-examination

You are so busy bringing up your children and managing your daily schedule that you have little time to reflect on the sort of example you set for your child. When you have a moment, do think about how you present yourself, what you look like, how you behave and the language you use in front of your child. Be prepared to change if you realize that some of the things you say and do possibly set a bad example for him. You cannot reasonably expect your child to behave at a more acceptable level than you! And if you see your child behave in a way that you dislike, first consider the possibility that he has already seen you do this. Such self-examination can lead to improvements in your child and yourself!

Single parents

Parents who raise their children single-handedly often worry that their child misses out on a same-sex or opposite-sex role model. This usually concerns mothers whose sons are brought up without a father at home, whether because of bereavement, divorce or life choice. Yet psychological research reveals that

Not surprisingly, parents are strong role models for their children, and it is worth considering what sort of model you make.

children of single parents are no more prone to emotional or psychological difficulties than children in two-parent families. So single parenting doesn't mean that your son will automatically lose out by not having a father role model at home. However, if you are concerned about this, try to arrange for him to spend time with other trustworthy, caring male adults in your own family. Maybe his uncle can take him out to watch a soccer match or perhaps he could attend a leisure activity run by a responsible male whom you feel provides a good role model.

Teaching by example

Here are some suggestions for you to help your child learn positively from the example you set:

Communicate openly and directly with your child. This sends a message that it is okay for her to be open and direct back.

♡ **Be self-aware** Be conscious of the things you say and do in front of your child, and don't be surprised when you see your mannerisms and attitude reflected in him. If you would prefer him to behave differently, change yourself first of all.

♡ **Communicate openly** He is more likely to be open and direct with you if that is the way you are with him. Make good communication a key part of your relationship with your child; teach him to express what he feels to you instead of bottling it up.

♡ **Express your joy of life** Life is for living, so let your child see that you take life seriously but that you also know how to enjoy yourself. Demonstrate how it is perfectly possible, with a little planning, to achieve a satisfactory work–life balance.

♡ **Show your stress-management strategies** Your child can learn how to manage stress by copying the techniques that you use. That is why it is good to explain to him how you try to problem-solve and prioritize when you go through episodes of pressure and stress.

♡ **Demonstrate your decision-making skills** Indecision is often linked to unhappiness. The example you set for your child when it comes to making decisions – by explaining the way you make choices – will empower him to act more decisively himself when the time arises.

♡ **Teach in manageable 'lessons'** In trying to act as a good role model for your child, be careful that you don't overburden him with too much information. Some situations are too complicated for him to grasp. Develop his understanding at a pace that he can cope with.

♡ **Monitor other role models** Bear in mind that your child is also influenced by other role models in his world, such as his teacher or a media personality (real or acting). Keep an eye on these other role models to ensure that they share your values.

Friends matter

It is highly beneficial for your child to have friends. She probably has more fun with friends than she has on her own – a group activity is usually more enjoyable than being alone. And she feels good knowing that she has friends. Friendships also help her through difficult times.

Individual sociability

Bear in mind that not every child has the same need to have friends or has the same ability to be sociable. So don't worry needlessly if your child is one of those who has only a couple of friends, while the child next door is the life and soul of the party. Almost certainly your child is happy with her level of sociability, and if you keep telling her to make more friends, you will end up making her feel that there is something wrong with her. To reassure yourself, subtly check out whether or not she would prefer to have a greater circle of friends. If she tells you that she would like to be more sociable, help her achieve this, but if she says that she is happy with her current social life, then leave well alone.

Facts about friendship

- Children whose parents are shy and have few friends tend to be shy themselves and have few friends; there is often a family pattern of sociability.
- Friendships between four- or five-year-olds often change from one day to the next; peer relationships becomes more stable from the ages of ten or 11 years old.
- Children usually have strong friendships with someone of their own sex up until the age of eight or nine; after that, opposite-sex platonic friendships can develop.
- Your child's best friend is probably like her in age, abilities and personality. We are usually friendly with people like us, although opposites can attract.

Friendly by nature

Children are, by nature, social animals – they have an innate tendency to interact with each other. Although this psychological need to belong, to be part of the group, varies from child to child and changes with age, she will generally be happier with friends than when alone. The importance of friendships heightens from the age of seven or eight years, and by the time your child is 12 years old, her friends play a very important part in her life.

Friends are an essential part of happiness; If your child has a couple of good friends, that is all that matters.

Q My child seems terrified whenever she has a slight fall-out with a friend. It's as if she is afraid of being socially isolated. Is that a normal reaction?

A You know that friendships come and go, but your child still has to learn about fair-weather friends. On the other hand, she also has to learn that good friendships can survive minor disagreements; indeed, they are often stronger afterwards. Try to find out whether your child's social position is as vulnerable as she thinks – perhaps all your child needs is reassurance that the situation is not so serious. Relationships between girls are often volatile, and what seems a social crisis one day is forgotten the next.

Q I don't approve of my seven-year-old's friend because they always get into mischief together. What should I do?

A Handle this very tactfully. If your child thinks that you want to stop her playing with her friend, this may push their relationship into secrecy, which would make it harder for you to influence. Take a two-pronged approach. Firstly, don't encourage your child to arrange play opportunities with her friend. Try to postpone their social activities or even cancel them. Secondly, specifically nurture the formation of new friendships for her, for example, by arranging to take your child and someone else from her class on an outing. The friendship that you disapprove of will become less intense in time.

Popularity

There is a link between your child's personality and his ability to make friends. While popularity depends to some extent on natural traits beyond most children's control, it also relies on other social skills that are within your child's reach to learn.

Social characteristics

Charisma, physical attractiveness, athletic and sports ability, leadership skills and a sense of humour are all innate attributes that influence popularity. However, research has identified other key, social characteristics that make a child popular with others – see the chart opposite. If your child already has these abilities, encourage him to use them with his peers, and if he lacks them, help him to acquire them.

Negotiation and compromise

It is one thing to make friends, but it is another to keep them. In any friendship, conflict occasionally arises, and your child's ability to resolve disagreements effectively will largely determine whether or not they stay friends. Two key skills needed for maintaining positive peer relationships and resolving social disputes are:

Negotiation When conflict arises between friends, it is usually over a clash of aims. For instance, one wants to play a particular game on the computer, while the other would prefer to go out. What starts out as a mild difference of opinion can quickly escalate into a full-blown row that splits the relationship. If negotiation is brought into play at an early stage, the dispute will be sorted out before the situation becomes inflamed. Negotiation involves your child deciding what he wants to achieve, taking note of what his friend wants to achieve and then using persuasion to bring his friend's position closer to his. Practise this with your child. Give him advice on how to phrase his comments and arguments in order to persuade you gently round to his point of view.

Compromise Negotiation alone, however, isn't effective enough for conflict resolution. It is a starting point only. In most cases, both friends will have to modify their opinions steadily until they reach a

Popularity is based on a variety of factors, including athletic ability, but cooperation, verbal skills and a happy face also count.

Key **sociable** characteristic

What you can **do**

Cooperation His ability to cooperate with his peers, to play games with rules, to take turns in a game, to share possessions and to listen to what other children say to him affects friendships.

Develop his ability to cooperate at home by playing games with him that involve turn-taking and sharing. Give him and his sister a small job to complete together, and encourage them each to do their fair share.

Spoken language Peer friendships operate mainly through spoken language. Good communication oils the wheels of social interaction, even in childhood.

Encourage him to talk to his cousins, for instance, when they visit. Teach him the art of making 'small talk' when with others, for example, by asking, 'What's your favourite television programme?' He will then transfer this skill to other contexts.

Body language Nobody wants to spend time with a child who looks sad, with shoulders drooping and a frown on his face – that body language conveys his discomfort and unhappiness.

Teach him to use positive body language when in a social situation. A smile on his face, his shoulders held high and good eye contact all create the image of a confident, friendly child. His peers want to be with someone who at least looks as if he is having a good time.

Sensitivity Nobody likes a child who thinks only of himself, who is rude and makes hurtful comments and whose temper is easily triggered by the slightest thing not going his way.

Give your child lots of praise when he acts sensitively and caringly towards a friend. If he is quick-tempered, explain why it is important for him to keep control of his anger. Never laugh at any rude remarks he makes or at any of his rude gestures.

common point that they are both comfortable with. Your child might find this difficult to master at first. He may prefer to hold his original ground because he doesn't see any reason why he should modify his expectations, or he may think that compromise is the same as giving in. Explain to your child that compromise involves both him and his friend changing their ideas in some way so that they both

come away from the dispute with a feeling of satisfaction. Give him examples of how compromise might turn out, and encourage him to consider the benefits to both parties.

Learning these key social skills of negotiation and compromise during this period of childhood provides a solid basis for him to use them further during the teenage years and indeed in adulthood.

Play with care

Not only is play the main means by which children learn, particularly before they start school, it also continues to be the most significant focus of social interaction for many years after that. Through play, your child can hone his caring attitude and sharpen his social skills.

Toys and behaviour

A research project examining the link between toys and behaviour required children to play in pairs. Six toys were provided, three 'aggressive' (space villain doll, mechanical boxing robot, warship) and three 'pro-social' (a ball and hand-held hoop, a peg-board that needed two children to operate it, a toy ambulance). The researchers found that children were more considerate to each other when playing with the pro-social toys (for instance, they cooperated and took turns) and were more anti-social to each other when playing with the aggressive toys (for example,

they were verbally abusive and sometimes even physically combative). Evidence like this underlines the importance of choosing toys and games very carefully. Make a list of the toys, computer games and board games that your child has and then divide them into 'pro-social' or 'aggressive'. You may be surprised by what you find!

Cooperative play leads to less conflict than competitive play. Your child will benefit from both types of play.

The role of super-heroes

Many children express their imagination through pretend-play as a super-hero, whether an all-powerful soldier, a champion fighter or an unbeatable character from a computer game. That is perfectly healthy and can be an important part of playing with friends. But there is no harm in encouraging him to pretend-play a less malevolent character who doesn't fight aggressively with everyone around him. Point out that he could imagine himself as someone who saves people from dangerous crises; not all super-heroes have to carry weapons of death and destruction. Your child can role-play someone who is kind and helpful to others just as easily as someone who is frightening and aggressive.

Competitive or cooperative play

Your child can be fiercely competitive in play even with his best friend. He wants to be the best whenever he can, and he probably wants to win at every game — for something that is supposed to be fun, play can be seriously competitive! Your child won't be the first one ever to have fallen out with his closest friend over a dispute about who won a game. Consideration often takes second place to victory in children's play. Help him to avoid competitiveness in play becoming so all-consuming that winning every game is all that matters to him. Of course you want your child to succeed, but not at any price.

Some children have difficulty playing games involving cooperation, such as building something together, because they are so used to playing competitively. They may grow agitated and tearful when they realize that they need to cooperate with another child. This type of frustration is normal. Just give lots of reassurance, for instance, 'Don't worry, you'll be able to play the game properly if you help each other'. If you consistently take that approach, you'll find that arguments in play become less frequent.

? QUESTIONS & ANSWERS

Q My ten-year-old is too caring in play — I have seen him deliberately lose a game just so that his friend feels happy. How can I make him tougher?

A Allow him to make this choice, as long as you are sure that he does it because he wants to and not because he is being forced into it. There is no reason why he should change if caring for others is his natural way of interacting. Look on this as a positive quality, to be admired. If your ten-year-old starts to feel differently in the future, he will change his behaviour of his own accord.

Q Even though I don't allow my eight-year-old to play with guns at home, that's the first toy he grabs at his friend's house! Why does he do that?

A Nobody knows for certain why children — especially boys — are so attracted to toy weapons. You have made a decision not to allow such toys at home, but that hasn't quelled his interest in them altogether. If you forbid him to play with them when he is with his friend, you will make them even more attractive in his eyes. Remember that occasional play with toy weapons is unlikely to encourage his aggression.

POSITIVE PARENTING

Having fun together

There is no doubt that parenting is hard work, yet it should also be good fun. Amidst all the stressful moments, the worries, the arguments and the challenges, there ought to be plenty of purely pleasurable times when you and your child just get on with enjoying each other's company.

Making time

You can't have fun with your child unless you are together – you need to make time to be together. This isn't always easy; after all, the typical school-age child is totally involved in preparing for school when she gets up in the morning, is then at school for a large part of the day and when she comes homes she is so tired that she slumps in front of the television set, music player or computer. On top of that, she probably has homework and maybe a drama class or sports class a couple of times a week after school. And then there is your own work-home schedule that may clash with your child's arrangements. The net effect is that quality time together is at a premium. Be determined, therefore, to spend relaxation time with her every day, if possible, but certainly at least a couple of times a week. If you don't make the effort, the chances are that it won't happen.

Range of activities

Having fun together doesn't necessarily mean going on expensive, elaborate trips or holidays – that would be fun, but the activity doesn't need to be so grand. You could play a game, go for a walk, watch a DVD, shop in the supermarket, draw or paint, visit the park, reminisce, dance, role-play, tell jokes – in fact, anything can be fun if you are together and you have the right attitude. Approach these shared opportunities positively, pushing irritations and other tasks and concerns to one side. She knows when you are enjoying her company, and that makes the experience more emotionally rewarding for her too. When that happens, her happiness level soars!

How to have fun

You can help to maximize the amount of fun you have with your child or children by following the suggestions below. At the same time, bear in mind that she also needs time to have fun with her friends. Peer interaction remains important for your child, so balance the time she needs for her friends with your time together.

♡ **Block out negatives** Don't think about the disagreement you had with her earlier in the day. Put negative thoughts to one side and concentrate only on what is happening between the two of you at this very moment.

♡ **Avoid interruptions** Once the two of you have embarked on something enjoyable together, try not to get diverted on to something else. Let the phone ring or the doorbell go unanswered.

♡ **Be yourself** Different people have different ways of expressing happiness, so don't think that you have to laugh loudly all the time or chuckle at everything your child says. Do what comes naturally to you. Be real, not contrived.

♡ **Gauge your child's reaction** Make sure that she is having fun too. Don't just assume that she is enjoying herself because you are having a good time. Monitor her responses subtly so that the two of you are in tune with each other.

♡ **Act spontaneously** Seize any opportunity for having fun with your child. The fun moment may have been unplanned, but you should always grab any chance for enjoyment as soon as you spot it.

You can model cooperative play and have fun together at the same time by joining in a game of cards or a boardgame.

Fun things to say

Here are five things you can say to your child to generate a sense of fun when interacting with her – she will love to hear you say these things, even if she doesn't respond immediately:

• 'This is such good fun. I really enjoy being with you.'

• 'I'm having a great time and I hope you are too.'

• 'This is so good – I'm already looking forward to the next time.'

• 'You're such a wonderful child; I'm having a fantastic time with you.'

• 'I'm really happy when we are together like this, and I can see you are as well.'

Beating social rejection

You will hurt deep inside if your child comes home from school one day, or from a birthday party, and admits to you, 'They don't like me; most of them hate me'. Social rejection is one of your child's worst nightmares; it makes him feel totally miserable. He wants to fit in with the gang.

One friend is enough

Research has found that having even just one friend helps to reduce feelings of isolation and loneliness in a child who is socially excluded, so even if some children don't like him, there will be others who do. Of course you must take your child's claims of social difficulties seriously, but don't over-react. In any case, point out to him that popular children are not always the nicest individuals – they might be popular not because they are nice but merely because they are good at sports or are physically attractive.

Cliques

Sometimes a small group of children form a clique, that is, a closed social group. Cliques are most common among school-age children. Although some cliques are harmless (for instance, children who share a taste in music), many small, close-knit social groups have a negative quality. At best, most children outside the clique feel awkward in its presence, and at worst, children in a clique make fun of the others in a deliberate attempt to socially reject them. If your child finds himself on the receiving end of a clique's social venom – for example, when he approaches them in the school playground – you may be best to advise him to steer clear of that group of children completely.

Finding solutions

For every social problem, there is a social solution, and you will have to work together with your child to find one that suits. If he complains that he has no friends, check out if there is a specific incident that has triggered this difficulty and help him to find ways to make the situation better. Remember that children's friendships in this age group are fragile at the best of times, and therefore what appears to be a serious social challenge one day might have much less emotional significance in a day or two.

LEFT AND BELOW Rejection at any age is painful and when it happens to your child it is deeply hurtful. But if he or she has one good friend, that can be enough. Try to find a solution to this problem, before your child loses all confidence.

? QUESTIONS & ANSWERS

Q My child has just confided in me that he is bullied in school. What should I do?

A Listen to his side of the story, let him know that you will do something to resolve the pressure he is under and monitor the situation for a week or so. When he comes home from school each day, ask him about any incidents of bullying. If you think there is a pattern of victimization that goes beyond a single isolated incident, persuade your child to allow you to involve his teachers. Reassure him that you will do this discreetly.

Q My child's best friend has fallen out with him. How can I help?

A The break-up of a close friendship can be very upsetting for children, especially as they approach the teenage years. One strategy is to encourage your child to find a way to heal the rift between them. Another is for him to accept that this friendship is over and to invest emotionally in new peer relationships. Your child will find it hard to let go of the friendship he valued, but that may be the only way forward.

Q Why does my eight-year-old never get invited to any of his classmates' parties?

A Look at his body language, social skills and use of language; the solution could lie in improving the way he relates and behaves towards others. In addition, consider the strategy of actively encouraging new friendships, for instance, by arranging a good child-centred outing to which he can invite someone from his class. He can gradually build new social connections step by step.

Words not actions

Children who are able to express their emotions honestly and accurately through spoken words instead of through physical actions tend to get on better with their peers – relationships are less strained and more positive. In addition, emotional fluency also results in less conflict, largely because difficulties are aired and then resolved at a very early stage.

Differences between the sexes

Children who are verbally fluent are usually happier and more settled than children who keep their feelings all bottled up inside them; there is no doubt that if your child can say what she feels rather than hiding her feelings, she will feel happier and less frustrated. Girls are typically better at talking than boys, but that probably doesn't surprise you! They make their first sounds at an earlier age, they say their first word sooner than boys and typically they have superior vocabulary, language structures and grammar. Girls also use a broader vocabulary in relation to emotions than boys, and therefore have the building blocks for good, verbal emotional expression. It is therefore understandable that girls are more able than boys to discuss their feelings. In comparison, boys are often reluctant to say what is going on inside, and are more inclined to express their tension, confusion and frustration through physical violence than through words; they may even think that a boy who uses language to demonstrate his sensitivity is effeminate.

Emotional fluency helps

Studies have found that a child with a weak ability to communicate her emotions to others is more likely to become involved in disruptive behaviour and petty delinquency, to feel dissatisfied with herself, with her achievements and with her family life, to have a lower level of personal happiness and a poor level of self-confidence. True, some children are naturally quieter than others, but that is a reflection of their personality, not of their ability to express their emotions – fortunately, they can communicate their feelings through words when they want to. As your child grows, encourage her to increase her 'emotional vocabulary'; by the age of 11 or 12 years, she is able to use more adult words.

Your child will find acceptance with her peers if she can express her emotions verbally rather than by physical actions.

What you can **do**

Try to build in discussions about feelings as part of your daily routine with your child. Through everyday experience of verbalizing her feelings to you, she will quite naturally adopt the same approach when she is with her friends.

When your child does express her emotions through words, do your best to react in a way that will encourage her to do so again. Your positive response reinforces her use of language.

Even if your child is 11 or 12 years old, she remains influenced by the examples you set for her. It helps her develop her expressive skills if you tell her your feelings about particular events, as that builds up her understanding and vocabulary of the words associated with feelings.

Remember that your child needs to externalize a whole range emotions through spoken language, not just positive (happiness, pleasure, confidence) but negative (sadness, disappointment, loneliness) too.

Her ability to be verbally expressive about feelings improves by having empathy for other children's emotions. The more insight she has into the emotional states of others, the more likely she will be able to analyse her own.

What you can **say**

Ask questions about the experiences she has had that day with a focus on her emotional response, such as, 'How did you feel when that happened to you today?'

Show that you are listening to her and ask appropriate questions, for example, 'I'm so interested to hear you say that – tell me more.' Also respond with remarks that demonstrate your interest.

After a shared activity, such as watching a movie, tell her how you responded to it emotionally, for instance, 'I had mixed feelings about the film. It was quite funny and uplifting at first, but then it made me sad in a depressing way.'

Where possible, encourage your child to express honestly and openly both negative and positive feelings by saying, for example, 'It's okay to tell me what you really think and feel, even if you have unpleasant feelings.'

You might suggest that she thinks about what her friend might be feeling when they talk together by saying, 'I'm sure your friend would like to share her feelings with you.'

Coping with conflict

The automatic tendency for many children is to raise their hand against anyone who annoys them. Make it clear to your child that hitting others as a result of conflict is unacceptable – he should express his rage through words, not violence.

Understanding consequences

Encourage your child to recall instances when he was on the receiving end of physical aggression and to tell you what he felt like during that episode. Explain the practical consequences of using aggression to sort out disagreements with his friends – for example, they will start avoiding him if he gains a reputation for hitting out. Once your child realizes that words are better than fists, teach him things to say so that he has an effective alternative to lashing out. This helps him learn that words are more effective than actions.

Assertiveness

When faced with conflict, your child has a better option than 'fight-or-flight' – assertiveness, which includes the ability to express a point of view firmly during a conflict, without generating further hostility. It is your child's capacity to stand up for himself, and to state his opinion confidently and clearly without offending the listener. An assertive child is one who is able to tell another, 'No, I can see that you want me to do this, but I would prefer not to', and if he can say this with a smile and a calm positive voice, so much the better.

Have your say

Negotiation, compromise and assertiveness are effective strategies for coping with conflict, but they only work if your child and his friend actually listen to each other – and most children are not very good at that. Genuine listening means actually giving the other person a chance to speak, whereas children in a dispute tend to speak over anyone they don't want to hear. Teach your child that he should give his friend time to say what he wants to say. Practise listening skills at home so that he is ready to use them when necessary in the outside world.

Describing conflict

Another technique for coping with conflict with peers is, firstly, to describe the problem verbally, secondly, to put a possible solution into words and, thirdly, to ask for the other child's opinion. This staged approach for coping with conflict doesn't always work, but it is a lot better than swinging fists at each other.

Teach your child that physical agression is never the answer to the situation. Help her learn to use words to resolve conflict.

QUESTIONS & ANSWERS

Q Should I fight my child's battles for him or should I let him fend for himself?

A If you fight all your child's battles for him, on the plus side, he will remain more sheltered from the stresses and strains of everyday social life in school and in the playground. He knows you are always there to step in on his behalf the moment conflict looms on the horizon. On the minus side, he will never have the opportunity to learn how to cope with conflict on his own, and your child will in consequence experience difficulty handling disputes when you are not there with him.

Q What's the effect on my child of seeing my partner and I quarrelling with each other?

A If your child stumbles upon the two of you in the midst of an argument – and it's important that you keep your rows within civilized bounds – reassure him that it's only a small disagreement. Tell him that you always get over these minor episodes. Anyway, he needs to learn that people do disagree sometimes and that it's normal to express anger. When he sees that you both argue but that you still love each other, he will come to understand that you can be annoyed with someone and still love that person at the same time. While it's never good for your child to see you rowing, infrequent fights in front of him need not be psychologically harmful when handled properly.

Bullying

Bullying is a menacing reality for some children, most commonly when they are at school. The victim is typically chosen because he is different from the main group, perhaps due to his size, style of speech or ethnic origin. Bullying has serious effects on a child's self-esteem and happiness.

Understanding bullying

Bullying is an abuse of power in a relationship in which one person (the bully) is perceived as strong, threatening and dangerous by the other (the victim). It is the perception of power that matters. The weaker child construes the bully as stronger, and it is this perceived imbalance of power that enables the dominant child to take command – in many instances, a bully is actually physically smaller than the target of his abuse. Malicious intent towards others is one of the hallmarks of the genuine bully.

Types of bullying

Bullying can take many different forms. A child can bully without actually laying a finger on his victim – threatening the victim verbally, or even hinting to the victim that he may be the focus of unpleasantness is a form of bullying. Common types of bullying include:

Physical force Punching or slapping, pushing forcefully, jostling, poking, kicking, tripping and snatching the victim's possessions away from him.

Extortion The bully demands, for example, money from another child and threatens him with a beating if he does not cooperate.

Verbal abuse Teasing a child about his appearance or about his disability, taunting a child about his friends or his parents or threatening to harm him.

Racial harassment Racially motivated attacks that are either physical, verbal or psychological.

Differences between the sexes

Girls are as likely as boys to experience bullying. However, there are differences between the sexes in the type of bullying that occurs. For example, boys tend to be more physically violent, whereas girls tend to favour verbal abuse, teasing and social exclusion. Bear in mind, though, that both types of bullying are equally painful to the victim. There are very few recorded instances of girls physically bullying boys (although some boys will bully girls), yet there have been incidents of verbal abuse from girls to boys.

How to help combat bullying

There are various steps you can take to help your child deal with instances of bullying. First of all, treat complaints of bullying seriously. It will have taken a lot of courage for your child to admit to you that he is being bullied, and he will be terrified in case the bully finds out. Reassure him that you will keep the matter entirely confidential.

Try to persuade your child to walk away whenever the bully moves towards him. Too often this

type of avoidance strategy is mistakenly construed by the victim as an act of cowardice and weakness, when in fact it really is quite sensible. Another effective strategy is for him to show as little reaction as possible to the bully. Teasing and bullying often stops when the intended victim displays indifference to the actions against him. Ignoring verbal and physical threats is difficult, but it can be done successfully. Suggest that he stays with a group in the playground. Bullies tend to target children who seem weak and isolated, and therefore a child standing alone in the school playground increases his or her vulnerability. In any event, resist the temptation to advise your child to retaliate. Firstly, he could end up with a severe beating, and secondly, if you advocate aggression, he might conclude that this is a good way to deal with all problems.

Many instances of school bullying can only be effectively dealt with by school staff, so talk to them about the problem. All schools have an anti-bullying policy, so you can expect to receive a sympathetic response – and help – when you let the teachers know what is going on.

The effects of bullying on children can be very damaging. Intervene as soon as you discover that your child is being bullied.

Signs of school bullying

- Your child is afraid of attending.

- He resists when you try to take him.

- He complains to you that he hates school.

- He has a sore stomach and a headache when going to school.

- He has unexplained bruises, cuts, grazes or scratches on his face, hands or legs.

- He frequently tells you that he has lost his school bag, lunch-box or books.

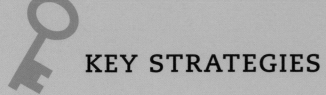

KEY STRATEGIES

Stress-busting

There so many potential stress points in your child's life – moving house, starting school, preparing for a test, falling out with her friends or not being invited to a party, to name just a few – that it is hardly surprising that she has moments when it is too much for her and she dissolves into tears.

Everyone is different

The perception of stress is very individual – what increases psychological pressure for your child might be seen as an exciting opportunity by her friends, and what she perceives as a major problem may appear insignificant to you. Remember, though, that your child's stress is real and that she needs your support.

What you can do

Here are ten stress-busting strategies to help you support your child through those emotionally charged periods that are part of growing up:

O– Opt for optimism, not pessimism Take an upbeat approach when your child is under stress. If you look anxious, she will become even more stressed herself. Your optimism at her ability to read aloud in class tomorrow is infectious and will encourage her.

O– Show you are there for her When your child feels stressed, her happiness level can be lifted to some extent just from knowing that you want to make her feel better. Explain that you want to help her sort out, for example, the disagreement she might be having with a friend.

O– React in good time You need a balance between helping your child before stress builds up and holding back to let her develop her own coping skills. Yet there is no point in leaving her to manage alone if the situation is already beyond her.

O– Identify the cause Work with her to pinpoint the source of stress. Sometimes the cause of your child's upset is obvious (for example, her brother constantly teases her), but in other cases the pressure point may not be so obvious.

O– Adopt an analytical approach Don't be put off when she insists that there is nothing troubling her, even though you can see that she is stressed. Instead, gently but systematically talk her through all the different areas of her life until you uncover the root problem.

O– Encourage positive communication Despite her reluctance when you try to engage her in discussion about her concerns, she will feel better after sharing her worries with you.

O– Suggest solutions Offer tangible and practical suggestions to your child about how to deal with whatever stresses her. For instance, you could help her draw up an exam revision timetable that includes scheduled breaks and relaxation time.

O—ᴇ Encourage anticipation Lack of control heightens stress. Therefore, encourage her to plan ahead in order to avoid potential problems. For example, regular practice will help her prepare for the next piano exam.

O—ᴇ Draw on past experience Mention previous episodes when she was stressed about a problem and yet she still managed to handle the pressure. Talk to your child about the strategies she used on that earlier occasion – they may be useful this time too.

O—ᴇ Evaluate success Once the stress has eased, chat with her about the methods she used. Through discussion, highlight those techniques that worked for her and those that were less effective. Encourage her to think about why they were successful.

Life can be hard for a child. Knowing that you are there, that you love him and that tomorrow is another day will help.

Stress statistics

Surveys suggest that one in five children experience stress to such an extent that it interferes with learning, friendships and happiness. Susceptibility to stress is increased by risk factors such as parental conflict, erratic discipline at home and poor housing. However, a child who has a warm, emotional bond with at least one parent is more resistant to the stresses of everyday life.

Positive communication

Speaking Out

By the time your child reaches school age, he is expected to be able to speak confidently to his peers, to school staff and to friends and family. Sometimes he needs to talk to one person, other times to a small group of people and on occasions to his whole class.

Opportunity knocks

If your child is a confident speaker, he will be delighted to have any opportunity to express his opinions and feelings to anyone who will listen, and each time he has a successful discussion, he will be even happier with himself. But if he has doubts about speaking out, he will dread those moments when this skill is required and he will be totally miserable each time his public-speaking performance is lacklustre. Being able to speak confidently will boost his happiness.

Ask the family

The best place for your child to learn to speak confidently is at home, through family discussions. There are ample opportunities for this to take place, for example, when chatting to him on a one-to-one basis about school, when discussing a topic with your entire family while eating the evening meal together and when he meets his cousins, aunts and uncles at occasional family gatherings. All of these experiences will develop his speaking skills, boost his confidence and encourage him to feel secure when talking to others. Almost certainly, this ability will transfer comfortably to other contexts.

Unfamiliar faces

One of the most difficult challenges for your child to cope with is speaking to unfamiliar children or adults. This can happen when, for example, he joins a new after-school activity class that has other children his age whom he has never met before, or when you meet a work colleague while out with him. He may find that the words simply don't flow and that he stands in embarrassed and involuntary silence. Practise these situations with him – teach him to make eye contact, smile, face the speaker and to reply with short sentences that indicate he is listening and wants to connect with them. Once he gets over this initial phase, his confidence in speaking confidently will have been established.

Class presentations are common in many schools, so encourage your child in the art of speaking clearly and fluently in public.

What you can do

Instead of pressuring him into speaking to others, take a low-key approach to developing his public-speaking skills.

Seek your child's views on issues that matter to him. This forces your child to clarify his thoughts and to find the words to express his opinions clearly to you.

He may lack confidence in speaking to unfamiliar children and adults because he literally can't think of anything to say in order to start the conversation, so teach him how to make 'small talk'.

Put your child in a situation where he is typically and routinely required to talk to others, but in a controlled and structured context.

Provide opportunities for your child to pay for items in shops. Explain that politeness usually receives a favourable response, but dissuade him from being discouraged if the sales assistant ignores him or is dismissive or bad-tempered.

How you can do it

Develop his ability to speak spontaneously, using experiences that arise naturally in everyday life. Asking him to chat to the shopkeeper, discussing with him the game he played with his sister and talking about what went on in school today all contribute to building up his speaking confidence.

Encourage him to make choices and to explain why he has made those particular choices. Although he may find this difficult at first, it will get him into the habit of speaking his views clearly and confidently to others.

Suggest specific 'small talk' openings to him, such as asking the child he has just met 'What's your name?' or 'How old are you?' Practise this with him regularly through role-play at home.

Enrol your child in a leisure activity class. The fact that all the children attending have a common interest means that there is an identified talking point right from the start. The adult supervision also ensures that there is structure and that he will be kept fully occupied.

Suggest ways for him to attract the sales assistant's attention and to ask for things politely. For example, he could say, 'Excuse me, please can you tell me where I can find...?'

Overcoming reluctance

We are, by nature, communicative – there is no doubt that human beings have an innate need to communicate with each other. That is one of the reasons why it is so frustrating when you know there is something troubling your child and yet she refuses to talk about it.

Barriers to communication

You desperately want her to talk to you so that you can help her sort out her problem, but she presents you with a stubborn wall of silence. Her happiness is at stake, but you quickly realize that the more you press her to express her inner feelings, the less she says. You can't force an explanation from her. Somehow, though, you have to break down this reluctance to speak and open the channels of communication. Here are some of the most common barriers that can inadvertently block the communication process between parent and child:

Physical Avoid possible distractions, so switch off background music and television. Position the furniture so that your child is beside you, not opposite or on the other side of a table. Do what you can to ensure that there are no interruptions, such as ringing doorbells and telephones. Lastly, make sure that you have privacy, away from other people.

Creating a relaxed environment may encourage your child to overcome his reluctance and talk to you more freely.

Psychological If you feel impatient with her silence, don't let it show or she will clam up even further. Sit calmly with her, even though there might be a hundred other activities that require your attention. Try to demonstrate that you treat her seriously and that you respect her concerns.

Try the loving touch

When your child is reluctant to speak to you, sometimes actions rather than words can break the communication impasse. A loving, physical gesture, such as taking her hand gently in yours, stroking her cheek softly or just placing your arm gently round her shoulders can help her feel more able to express her feelings. Don't be surprised if she starts crying in response – if she does, soothe her until she calms down. In some instances, a release of tears like this is necessary before there can be a release of words.

Once she does start to open up and talk to you, give her plenty of time to say what she wants. If your child found it easy to express herself verbally, she wouldn't have needed all that prompting from you in the first place. And remember that you can continue to use gentle touch even once she starts speaking, especially if you feel that this is effective.

Ten things you can say

Here are ten comments you can make to your child when she sits opposite you in silence, even though you know she would be happier talking to you. Using them may help to prompt her out of her reluctance to communicate. Through trial and error, you'll discover which strategy works best for your child.

1 'You're clearly restless and unsettled. Most children feel that way sometimes. Take as long as you want before you say what you want to tell me.'

2 'It can't be easy for you, what with the difficulties you are having with your friends. It might help you to talk to me about it, even for a few minutes.'

3 'We can sit here quietly together if you want. I enjoy your company and I don't mind at all if you'd prefer not to discuss anything with me.'

4 'The last time something troubled you, you didn't want to talk to me about it. However, you'll remember that you were a lot happier once we'd had a chat.'

5 'It's sometimes difficult to find the right words to say what you feel. It can happen to us all – we feel in a certain way, but we struggle to put that feeling into words.'

6 'You're such an enthusiastic child, so I know that when you are sad like this, something is worrying you. Maybe you can tell me about it?'

7 'Things can be very confusing at your age and you can have a problem trying to make up your mind. You'll find that sharing your problem with me will help.'

8 'I think you want to tell me something and I definitely want to hear what you have to say. So between us, we should be able to discuss it.'

9 'Sometimes children upset each other without actually realizing what they've done, without deliberately doing so. Maybe that's what has happened to you.'

10 'There is no problem that I can't help you with. Whether it's big or small, I'm here for you. We can chat now or later – whatever you want to do.'

Family meals

Having a family meal – that is, where all members of the family sit round a table to eat together – is sadly a rapidly fading part of family life. The family meal is a rich source of emotional and intellectual stimulation that can contribute to your child's happiness, confidence and well-being.

Re-instituting the family meal

Putting the family meal on or back on the agenda, and thereby reaping the social benefits, can be successfully achieved if you approach the matter in a systematic and proactive way:

♡ **Be determined to succeed** Once you have made up your mind to start having family meals, have sufficient determination to follow it through. Don't allow yourself to be dissuaded by your children's objections or the clash between your work rota and your partner or close family member or friend's schedule. Aim to succeed.

♡ **Pick a starting date** Once you have introduced the idea of the family meal to everyone, pick a starting date, say, one week from now. Tell them all well advance that this is going to happen and ask them all to make sure that they are available. Keep a positive attitude, and work on the assumption that it will be good fun.

♡ **Have realistic expectations** Sometimes the family meal will go well, with everyone thoroughly enjoying themselves, other times it will not go so well

Family meals are a great time to talk; let your youngest speak first so that she isn't drowned out by her older siblings.

because your children bicker with each other and on other occasions the experience will be somewhere in between. Don't expect too much from it.

♡ **Encourage conversation** You are more likely to keep everyone at the table for the full meal if they are engaged in lively conversation. Try to avoid silences, if possible – fill the gaps by asking suitable questions that involve others in discussion. They will all soon get the idea.

♡ **Target the youngest** The one who is probably least likely to take part in family discussions during mealtimes is the youngest, mainly because the older members of the family will generally get in first with what they have to say. So make a point of giving your youngest child the time and space to have his say.

♡ **Avoid distractions** Your family's focus during the meal will be stronger if their eyes don't wander towards the television or computer screen. Switch off the television or computer, or arrange the table so that the screen isn't in sight. Reassure them that they will cope without it for half and hour.

♡ **Involve him in preparation** Where possible, try to involve your child or children in some way in preparing for the family meal. It really doesn't matter what he or they do, as long as they are involved in the preparation; that increases their commitment to the experience.

♡ **Be persistent** The more you have family meals, the more your family will look on the occasion as part of the typical family routine, and the lure of competing attractions will steadily diminish.

Pros and cons of eating together

Reasons why family meals slide off the agenda:

• You all have competing work and leisure schedules.

• There is a very interesting television programme on at that time.

• Your child gets restless sitting at the table.

• There are often fights during family meals.

• You all prefer to eat different foods, at different times of the day.

• You are so tired at the end of the day that you would rather eat in silence.

• You don't have a dining table big enough for you all to sit together.

Reasons why family meals should definitely be on the agenda:

• They provide a good level of stimulation for your child.

• You all keep up to date with each other's lives.

• Meals involve turn-taking, sharing and listening.

• Tensions can be resolved during mealtimes.

• It is fun spending time with each other.

• Your children are able to talk to each other or to you.

• They allow your child to sharpen his communication skills.

Learning to listen

Your child might be good at talking, but that doesn't mean that she is good at listening! Sometimes you ask her to do something for you and she is slow to respond; at other times she appears not to hear you altogether. You need to encourage her to develop listening skills.

Why she isn't listening

There are a variety of reasons why your child doesn't appear to listen to what you have to say. Probably the most common of these is a competing attraction – if she is captivated by a programme on the television or her ears are filled with music from her ear-plugs, your voice has a hard task breaking through to her. You can't assume that she will automatically pick out your voice from all the other sounds. As your child grows up, she starts to think that she knows better than you, that what you have to say doesn't fit in with her plans. Consequently, her general strategy is to reject your suggestions, and so it seems as if she isn't listening.

On the other hand, always consider the possibility that it is not simply that your child hasn't listened to you, but that you have not explained your ideas properly. Perhaps there is another way you could express yourself more clearly. In the case of some children, their hearing ability can be affected by coughs and colds, so do take this into account. And if you have any doubts at all about your child's hearing, have it checked out by your family doctor. However, the chances are that her hearing is fine and that it's matter of her not listening to you, rather than not hearing you.

Can he talk but not listen? Ask your child to look at you and make eye contact before you start to speak.

What the **problem** is

Your child continues to do whatever she is in the process of doing, even when you are talking to her.

She seems to listen to what you have to say at the time, but then later forgets what you have said.

You tell your child clearly not to do something, but she ignores what you say and goes ahead and does it anyway.

She talks over you all the time, not listening whenever you are trying to say something to her, no matter how important.

What you can **do**

Your child cannot adequately listen to you unless she concentrates fully on what you have to say. So if you want her to pay attention, start off by saying her name and asking her to turn to look at you. Don't continue with what you have to say until you are making eye contact with her. Only then should you tell her what you want to say.

This difficulty usually occurs because either what you have told her is too complicated for her to remember, or she has lost interest halfway through and has stopped listening. A good strategy for improving retention is to ask your child to repeat what you have just said to her. Don't do this in a confrontational way; explain that you just want to check that she has fully understood what you said.

By the time your child is eight or nine years old, she knows that she is able to think for herself, which means that she is only a small step away from deciding to ignore your opinions. So explain clearly and calmly to her that in the same way that you value her opinions, you expect her to value yours, and just as she doesn't like being ignored by you, neither do you like being ignored by her.

Resist the temptation to talk over her in return, or you will both end up speaking louder and louder, with no one listening to anyone! Stop talking when she tries to talk over you, let her say what she wants and when she has finished start to speak again. In time, your child will learn that she cannot stop you expressing your ideas, even though she doesn't want to listen to what you have to say.

Privacy

You know that your child will be happier when she shares her life with you – when she doesn't keep secrets from you and when she confides her concerns in you. But maybe your child is more reserved, preferring to keep her feelings to herself.

Reasons for keeping secrets

Children keep secrets from their parents for a variety of reasons. Secrets can become an exciting part of her friendships; she enjoys having confidences that she shares only with her friends, for example, secrets about the music she likes or the teachers they dislike. Sometimes a child keeps a secret because she knows it concerns something her parents would disapprove of; she prefers concealment or even dishonesty to

facing parental reaction to the truth. And there are occasions when a child keeps a secret and won't confide in her parents because she has been asked to do so by a third party. While the first is benign, the last two instances are always cause for concern.

Managing confidences and secrets

Tell your child that you think it is acceptable for her to talk about her feelings in private with a friend. She shouldn't be made to feel guilty about that. However, explain that some things should never be kept secret, for example, if she is in danger of being hurt or if the secret involves something she knows is wrong.

Emphasize that she should never keep a confidence just because she is afraid of the consequences of revealing it to you. Make it clear to your child that she can talk to you about anything and that you will always listen to what she has to say. Add that you won't divulge her secrets. It is important to explain that you always want her to tell you the truth, even if that means admitting she has done something she knows you will disapprove of.

Probably the main worry you have when it comes to secrets is that your child might conceal something from you which you should really be made aware of, and it's very hard to know how far you should press her to reveal the information. If you are forceful with her, she may simply deny that there is any secret at all – and then you will never find out. Be honest with her about your concern. Tell your child upfront that you are worried she is hiding something from you and that you would prefer her to be direct and open about it. In the end, however, she will make her own choice.

Keeping a diary is a good way for older children to express themselves, especially if they are reserved about their feelings.

Q My 12-year-old has started keeping a private diary. Should I sneak a look at it when she is out at school?

A Although you are troubled by the appearance of the diary because you look on it as barrier between you and your child, it is simply her way of keeping a record of her personal thoughts. The diary enables her to 'voice' her feelings without fear of criticism or ridicule. There is nothing wrong with that – respect her privacy. Don't break the trust that lies in your relationship with her. She will be justifiably angry if she learns that you took advantage of her by peering into her diary when you knew she didn't want you to. Instead of underhand tactics, far better to be open and honest with your 12-year-old and tell her that you are afraid the diary means that the two of you won't talk as much as you did before, and seek her reassurance on this matter.

Q Our child is ten years old and she confides in me about absolutely everything. But I would rather she handled some situations on her own. What should I do?

A There's a fine line between a child sharing everything with her parents and actually relying on them too much to sort things out for her. An effective way to encourage your ten-year-old to keep you in the picture while avoiding over-dependency is to listen to her confidences and concerns without taking over. Make sure that she does the work herself. Therefore, instead of immediately offering solutions, ask your child questions that make her think more deeply about the situation. Direct her towards finding her own solutions.

POSITIVE PARENTING

Parents needs

If you are not happy because you feel your own needs are unfulfilled, then your child will not be happy either. To a large extent, his mood state reflects your own mood, and therefore if you are frustrated and sad for much of the time, he will begin to feel the same way too.

Identifying your needs

Meeting your needs as a parent is as important to your child's contentment as it is to your own. With the non-stop demands of parenting, with the constant requirement to attend to your child's need, the chances are that consideration about what you need to thrive is given low priority. In the long term, however, that approach will not have a positive outcome. You have a range of psychological needs, including the need to feel competent as a parent – to know that you are doing a good job in raising your child – and that partly derives from receiving positive feedback from your child or from others commenting on your parenting skills. Then there is your need to be loved by your child; the emotional attachment between you and your child is two-way. Bear in mind that you also have the need to develop as an individual, not solely within the parenting role but also socially and intellectually. Make sure that you don't simply concentrate on the parenting dimensions, with the resulting exclusion of all your other needs.

Take a positive approach

The most effective way to ensure that you are happy and fulfilled as a parent is to take a positive approach to parenting. This means having an optimistic attitude, developing purposeful strategies for raising your child and managing your role as a parent in an effective way so that you feel good about yourself. A positive approach to parenting also involves taking the initiative, planning ahead and regaining control of your life. This is easier said than done, of course, because living with a demanding child can reduce the confidence of even the most robust parent. But you can change your techniques as parent in order to make life better for you. If you feel good about yourself, this has a positive knock-on effect for everyone else in your family.

How to meet your own needs

There are various ways in which you can take positive action to ensure that you feel happy and fulfilled, both as a parent and an individual in your own right:

♡ **Resolve conflicts, not prolong them**
Fights between you and your child can last from one day to the next, or even longer, without ever being resolved. That is only going to reduce your parenting confidence. Instead, identify the root of the disagreement, then make a definite effort to resolve it. You'll both feel much better when you have put the dispute behind you.

Making time for yourself will help you to feel more relaxed and happy, which means your children will feel happy too.

♡ **Look for your strengths, not weaknesses**
When your child frequently misbehaves, it is easy to assume that you are doing something wrong and that it is all your fault. But that approach only leads you into a downward spiral. Focus on the parts of parenting that you are managing effectively.

♡ **Suggest changes, not apportion blame**
The pressures of living with a growing child who challenges and provokes at regular intervals can lead you into blaming him for your dissatisfaction. It is more helpful to move on by looking positively for ways to improve the situation.

♡ **Take help and support when offered**
Nobody says you have to do everything by yourself. Accept offers of help from your partner, your close friends or relatives – that is not a sign of parental inadequacy. And listen to advice; you don't have to do what others suggest, but there is no harm in listening.

♡ **Take control; don't be passive** Raising a child takes over your life, especially when things don't go smoothly. You end up spending all your waking hours worrying, and you may feel that there is nothing more you can do. Don't be passive, but take control and make positive choices about the way you manage your child.

♡ **Make some 'me' time** Do your best to arrange time for yourself. This isn't about putting your needs ahead of your child's needs; instead, it is about recognizing that you need space to recharge your batteries. Occasional short periods on your own mean that you can return refreshed to be with your child. We all need a bit of self-indulgence occasionally, so don't feel guilty about that.

Using language positively

What you say to your child – and the way that you say it – has a huge impact on her. If you talk negatively towards her, perhaps giving a reprimand or expressing disappointment at her behaviour, the chances are that she will feel negatively about herself.

Choosing the right words

Conversely, if you speak positively to your child, for example, praising her achievements or commenting on her helpful behaviour, the likelihood is that she will feel more positively about herself. Of course, the link is not always clear-cut, but in general, positive parental language generates positive child emotions. That is why it helps to choose your words carefully when speaking to your child. Although she may appear not to listen to you at times, in most instances your choice of words directly raise or lower her happiness levels.

Positive criticism

Much as though you would probably like to talk positively to your child all the time, there will be moments when you have to let her know that you are not pleased with her. There is a place for criticism in your relationship with your child. What counts, however, is not the criticism itself but the context in which that difficult message is delivered. Positive criticism enables you to explain to your child what you don't like about her behaviour, while still leaving her in a positive frame of mind – that way you are happy because you get your point across and she is happy because she knows what she is doing right as well as what she is doing wrong.

Set criticism in the context of praise. For example, instead of saying 'I am annoyed at you for teasing your brother', you could say, 'I'm surprised at

you teasing your brother because normally you are so kind to him'. You can also include suggestions for change in your criticism, so instead of saying, 'You're so lazy for not finishing your homework', you could say 'I think it would be helpful if you and I arrange a manageable homework schedule for you'. Focus your criticism on your child's behaviour, not your child, by for instance saying, 'I didn't like what you did to your friend because it wasn't very thoughtful', rather than, 'You're very thoughtless for doing that to your friend'.

A hug, a compliment or an 'I love you' will have a big impact on your child. Everyone needs approval, regardless of age.

What you can **say**

Simply say, 'I love you'. You may find that she shrugs this comment off, especially when she reaches school age, but rest assured that your comment has a big positive effect.

Tell her, 'You're wonderful'. You can make that comment generally, for instance, when you spend time together, or you can make it in response to something specific she has done.

On those inevitable occasions when she falls short of her target, explicitly acknowledge your child's efforts by saying, 'I know you've tried hard'. The next time she helps you with an everyday task, take the opportunity to express your heartfelt thanks for her efforts.

Be prepared to say 'thanks' to your child when she has made a particular effort to help you out, even though she doesn't say 'thanks' to you as much as you would like.

When it comes to deciding on a particular issue, such as what type of computer you should buy or a suitable bedtime for her, ask her, 'What's your opinion about that?'

Why say it

She has a basic emotional need to be loved, whether she is four years old or 12 years old. Your repeated verbal affirmation of the positive feelings you have for her gives her reassurance, makes her feel secure and raises her happiness.

Your child loves to hear that you think she is terrific – it adds to her feelings of self-worth. Knowing that her parents value her highly gives her a warm emotional glow, and her confidence is boosted.

She wants to succeed in all that she strives for, but help your child to recognize that, although the end result is important, the process leading to that point is also central. Giving a supportive comment when she doesn't fully accomplish a goal will enable her to channel her energy to overcome the temporary setback and to try again.

You help your child every day in many different ways, major and minor, without receiving thanks from her, and therefore it seems only reasonable that she should help you now and again without expecting you to thank her. Yet thanking her makes her feel very special and draws positive attention to her caring behaviour. As a result, she is more likely to do the same again in the future.

As she grows, your child is more able to form views and express opinions. If you specifically ask her to comment on an issue, what you are really telling her is that you respect her and value her contribution to the decision-making process.

Body language

Children (and adults) communicate with each other all the time without using words. Body language (also known as 'non-verbal communication') is the term used to describe the messages that are transmitted from one person to another simply by physical gestures, such as a smile or a frown.

Key to communication

Psychologists regard body language as an important part of communication. Spoken language only occurs when your child makes a decision to speak to you. However, his body language goes on all the time. Even when he is asleep, you can tell by looking if he is restful or having a bad dream. Non-verbal communication is very powerful – studies have revealed that in the typical parent-child relationship, emotions are expressed almost ten times more through body language than they are through spoken language. While your child makes a conscious effort to talk to you, his body language is less controlled and more spontaneous. In other words, he can stay silent but he can't turn off his body language, which means you can learn a lot from it. The more you get to know your child, the better you will become at reading his body language accurately. This greater understanding of each other helps strengthen the emotional attachment between you.

A way to express feelings

Psychologists estimate that in any conversation between parent and child, over half the meaning is conveyed non verbally. And closer analysis of parent-child conversations demonstrates that children typically use words to communicate facts and ideas, whereas they typically use body language (deliberately or involuntarily) to convey emotions. Therefore body language is a very useful mechanism in any

interaction for expressing feelings to someone else. You can encourage your child to use non-verbal communication to improve relationships with his peers. With a little effort and concentration, he can learn positive body language.

Encouraging positive body language

First impressions count when children meet each other, and therefore confident body posture, strong eye contact, a warm facial expression and a relaxed manner all help your child make new friends. You can increase his awareness of these aspects of his body language with him at home so that he feels comfortable using them in social contexts. Once the friendship has been formed, encourage him to continue using body language positively, although in more subtle ways, including:

Attentiveness This is more than just making steady eye contact – after all, that can appear intimidating or insincere. Attentiveness is about occasional and regular eye contact that drifts away from the other child for no more than a couple of seconds at a time – if he looks away longer than that, he will appear bored. He should also moderate his facial expression in harmony with the speaker's mood so that he demonstrates that he is listening to the other child. This helps facilitate good communication.

Communications via positive body language help children make friends and forge bonds in a non-verbal way.

Positive reinforcement This involves your child using body language to show approval of something his friend has done, for example, a smile when his friend shares his sweets with him, or a thumbs-up gesture when he is pleased with the way his friend has helped him. Any physical sign of approval that he conveys to someone else is positive reinforcement. Research suggests that adults are more adept than children at using body language in this way, so expect the need to give your child encouragement.

Pacifying gestures These are aspects of body language that convey a sense of caring, helpfulness and non-aggression can be helpful for calming tension, avoiding conflict and generating a serene quality in a peer relationship. Pacifying gestures include movements such as clapping to indicate approval or happiness; extending a helping hand, for example, to pull his friend up or to pat him gently on the back; and sharing, which is a very strong non-verbal confirmation of friendship. The use of these gestures helps create a friendly, calming atmosphere and reduces potential tension. they can be useful in a range of situations whether your child is connecting with other his own age or with adults.

Positive communication   **121**

KEY STRATEGIES

Coping with change

Most children like their world the way it is, and they have little desire for change – excitement, yes, but change, no. A predictable routine, with familiar people and familiar surroundings, makes them feel safe and secure. Yet your child has to learn to cope with change, because change is an inevitable part of her world.

What you can do

You can help to minimize the negative effects of change on your child by managing the situation in various ways:

O⊨ Anticipate changes If you know change is coming in the near future, for instance, your child is due to leave one school to attend another or to end one leisure class to begin another, be aware that she may have adjustment difficulties, even if she is looking forward to the new event. Watch her reaction closely to identify any alterations in her behaviour that might indicate that she is worried or unhappy.

O⊨ Discuss impending change Talk to your child about any change that is in view. Encourage her to voice her excitements and her fears to you so that you are in tune with her feelings. Give her lots of reassurance that she will manage the transition without much difficulty, and that you will help her deal with any problems that might arise. Knowing her anxieties about what lies ahead enables you to resolve them more effectively.

O⊨ Make preparations for change Difficulty with change is often linked to fear of the unknown – your child isn't entirely sure of what the change will involve and therefore her stress levels rise. Avoid this aspect altogether by telling her in plenty of time what is involved in the new situation. Perhaps she can visit

When change is in the air – a new home or a new school – talk about it with your child, so that she can get used to the idea.

the new school or meet her new carer before the new arrangement actually takes place. All preparation in this way is helpful.

O⚊ Help her skill up for change Your child will be happier with change when she feels confident that she has the necessary skills. For instance, she won't be afraid to meet new children if she thinks that she is socially adept; and she won't worry about a new maths curriculum if she knows that she has good mathematical understanding. She will be much happier when she develops skills useful for dealing with the new situation.

O⚊ Acknowledge the difficulties she faces In some instances, such as a bereavement, there is nothing good about the change. But you can still facilitate your child's emotional adjustment by acknowledging her distress. Just letting her know that you are aware that she finds the circumstances very difficult can influence her ability to cope. Your psychological support will help her get through stressful emotional episodes in her life.

O⚊ Take a positive view Despite your child's possible anxiety about change, take a positive approach. Don't go out of your way to avoid change for fear it might upset her, as she will have no experience with which to develop her coping skills. Instead, suggest to her that she looks on change as an opportunity to progress and develop, not as a threat to her security and happiness. It is a matter of her switching perspective.

O⚊ Involve her in change She will be much happier about change when she feels connected to the process. That is why it is good to involve her in planning for change, wherever possible. For instance, she can take part in discussions about choosing the new family home or her new school. The more she

Help your timid child manage a change by involving her – visit her new school or talk about her bedroom in the new house.

participates in planning for change, the better she will cope with it when it arrives.

O⚊ Reflect on the change experience Once change has taken place, spend time chatting to your child about her reaction, about what she felt before and about how she feels now. Ask her if she thinks anything could have been done differently to make the change less challenging for her. Highlight 'lessons learned' from past experience and utilize them the next time. By encouraging this sort of personal reflection, your child increases her adaptability to changes in her surrounding. She recognizes effective coping strategies that she has used previously, which strengthens her ability to be content with change when it occurs in the future.

Getting along with others

Index

Acknowledgements

Executive editor Jane McIntosh

Editor Emma Pattison

Executive art editor Penny Stock

Designer Geoff Borin

Picture researcher Vickie Walters

Production controller Nigel Reed

Alamy/image100 41; /Steve Sant 94; /Janine Wiedel Photolibrary 64; /Jennie Woodcock/Bubbles Photolibrary 123
Corbis UK Ltd 11, 101; /Paul Barton 33; /Benelux/zefa 110; /Steve Chenn 108; /Jim Craigmyle 24; /Darama 17; /Peter Dazeley 77; /Kim Eriksen/zefa 85; /Grace/zefa 50, 53, 60, 62, 98; /Martin Harvey 90; /Alexander Hubrich/zefa 38; /Chris Jones 70; /Wolfgang Kaehler 44; /Ronnie Kaufman 73; /Yang Liu 104, 121; /Simon Marcus 21; /Markus Moellenberg/zefa 15; /Steve Prezant 29, 30; /Mark Seelen/zefa 35; /Ariel Skelley 8, 12; /Tom Stewart 95; /Larry Williams/zefa 118
Getty Images 20, 27; /Jenny Acheson 82; /Bruce Ayres 122; /Colin Barker 54; /Peter Cade 80; /Gary S. Chapman 103; /Nick Clements 88; /Robert E. Daemmrich 46; /Mark Douet 93; /Jan Greune 78, 96; /Sean Justice 69; /Lonny Kalfus 59; /don & liysa king 49; /Alex Mares-Manton 86; /Gustavo Di Mario 42; /Ebby May 67; /Nicholas Prior 106; /Didier Robcis 114; /Siri Stafford 117; /Stockbyte 74; /Titus 112; /Vast Photography 28; /Mel Yates 57; /Yellow Dog Productions 7, 16
Octopus Publishing Group Limited 14; /Vanessa Davies 4-5; /Adrian Pope 18, 58; /Peter Pugh-Cook 2, 19, 22, 26, 32, 36, 39, 40, 43, 52, 63, 84
Photodisc 10, 34